Jump Rocky Jump
How I Fell into Stunt Work

Rocky Taylor

Jump Rocky Jump
How I Fell Into Stunt Work

Pegasus

A CIP catalogue record for this title is
available from the British Library

ISBN-9781910903247

*Pegasus is an imprint of
Pegasus Elliot MacKenzie Publishers Ltd.*
www.pegasuspublishers.com

First Published in 2019

**Pegasus
Sheraton House Castle Park
Cambridge CB3 0AX England**

Printed & Bound in Great Britain

Author Rocky Taylor, 2019

Co-author Jon Auty, 2019

FOREWARD

BY RAY WINSTONE

'Rocky Taylor… the name alone sounds tough, like a heavyweight fighter. You could imagine him in the ring with many of the other great Rocky's in boxing history. Marciano and Balboa.

A tough man, you had to be back then just to get on.

And that's exactly what he is, but also much, much more.

Must have met Rocky around forty-three years ago. I was a young actor finding his way in a business I didn't know too much about. I have a feeling it was on TV we met the first time. An episode of The Sweeney if memory serves.

I didn't really have any friends who were actors – where I am from there weren't many people who really thought about going into the arts. People from my world when entering the arts would either become *sparks or stuntmen, so I was drawn towards them – they spoke my language.*

Men like Nosher, Dinny, Greg and Gary Powell, Terry Walsh – I could go on. Oh, and then Rock.

In a way Rocky and his little mob would always spoil a film for me. They were so recognizable that every time he would come on screen in a movie I knew there was going to be a fight or a car crash. Sure enough a few minutes after they appeared, all hell would break loose and the claret would start to flow.

Another reason why I tried to get him some of my pictures. Not only is he very professional and you feel safe and sound while he's around, but he's a mate and you like to have your mates round you when you work right? Sexy Beast was a great example. It was work yeah, but we had such fun. Days we spent chatting to each other under water in our pants! About, four years ago was the last time we worked together on a film on the Isle of Man called Ashes. I hadn't seen Rocky for a while, so it was good to catch up. We spent plenty of time in the evenings eating Chinese and drinking saki, talking about times gone by, the friends that are no longer with us, the ups and downs of life and our industry. I guess Rocky will talk about this in his own words, so I'll leave that to him – all I know is it has been an absolute pleasure knowing this gentle tough giant. A man amongst men. A man who is an artist who does a job that makes me and actors like me look good. A man I call my friend'.

Love yer Rock
Ray Winstone February 2018

PREFACE

A stuntman or stuntwoman typically performs stunts intended for use in a motion picture or dramatized television. Stunts seen in films and television include car crashes, falls from great height, drags (for example, behind a horse) and explosions.

That's what the dictionary has to say on the matter, but for me it's so much more. I've been incredibly lucky to work on many of the greatest movies of all time and to have met many of the great screen legends over the years.

I've had fights, rolled cars, crashed motorbikes, been knocked down, set on fire, fallen down stairs and jumped from tall buildings... and that was just on Monday! In the early days I was involved in everything. If a scene called for a double or a stunt of some shape or form, I'd get a call. To think that I would be pretending to die for a living and for fifty years... well you couldn't make it up. But it's true and that's why I decided to write this book. So many stories and so little time. I'm seventy-one next birthday and I'd like to be able to have something that documents my very unusual life.

I've visited so many wonderful countries, eaten the best food and drunk the finest wines. But I wouldn't have been able to do any of this without my friends, family and laughter.

Whilst you're on set in the studio or on location you always find time to laugh. You have to. It's one of those things that makes the day go by. On a film set you can be sat around for hours so you need that spark that gets you through the day. I mean, how boring would life be if you arrived at the office for instance and just did the work? You'd go mad within the first day and never go back for day two. That's why this business has characters.

Those individuals who make the most awful day the best you've ever had. The late great Roger Moore was a fine example of this. A natural actor with good looks, charm and comic timing you'd pay extra for. Some of his moments on set were legendary. For instance, he would always be looking for an excuse to catch the late Desmond Llewelyn, who played Q in the James Bond films, out whilst they were doing their scenes. Desmond would already have a page and a half of complicated jargon to learn whilst taking props and demonstrating how the gadgets worked to Bond. Roger would nip off to the script girl and get the dialogue changed, getting it presented to Desmond as though it had come from the director. Then, after Desmond had learnt the new words, Roger would stand in Desmond's eyeline and hold up signs with the word 'BOLLOCKS' written on it.

So next time you're sat in the cinema watching a thriller or action adventure try to put yourself in the stunt performer's position. Yes, he's just thrown himself from the horse galloping across the countryside and onto the back of a moving stagecoach, but twenty minutes before he was showing the wardrobe assistant his holiday snaps or the crossword.

Unbelievable attention to detail, the will to stay alive and the belief that for that moment on screen the stuntman is the hero.

It's a rush like no other and I wouldn't change it for the world.

Rocky Taylor
Surrey England
March 2018

THE EDGE

I stand at the bottom of a flight of wooden stairs. I climb. At the top I walk to my position. Standing there waiting is the worst part. I look around to make sure I'm standing in the right place. I walk to the edge and look down. I can see the landing area and the crowd of people that are standing behind the barriers.

"You ready, Rocky?" says an amplified voice from down there.

"Ready!" I shout back.

"Light the building." They are starting the fire. My heart starts to pump a little faster.

"Roll cameras." My mouth has gone dry. I won't be up here long though, so when I've done this, I can get something.

"Action!" Christ it's hot, I mean really hot. Why is it so big? The flames should just be small… how can I get to the edge if the fire is this big?

"Rocky?" Jesus… it's so hot. I'm getting out, this is way out of control. I've got to get over to the steps at the back, but where are they? I can't see the steps… I can't see the edge… I can't see anything.

"Go Rocky!" Think Rocky… come on, what am I going to do? I can't stay on here – this is dangerous. The edge, where is the edge? I got to go now or I'm going to die. Think, think… there, over there that's got to be where the landing area is. Fuck it… I've just got to jump.

"Jolly good."

It's quiet, no sound, no shouting. Why is there no sound? Wait, I can hear, oh Christ! Pain! So much pain! Oh no, SOMEBODY… AAAGGGGHHHHHHHHH!!!!!

HOW I JUST FELL INTO IT

Dad was away a lot working on pictures and I managed to get on the technical side of film making by studying clapper loading at British Films in Shaftesbury Avenue. I used to do it all in those days, make the tea, answer the phone and one day the switchboard rang. I inserted the headset into the line and said hello. A stunt coordinator called Peter Diamond called to ask me if I would help him out. How could I help out a stuntman?

He said, "I've been talking to your dad and he tells me that you are already a black belt in judo, so with that in mind I need a favour. Would you be able to take an actor down to the gym and show him a few judo moves and falls, so he can prepare for a fight we're going to do?"

I thought about it for a moment and said, "Who's the actor?"

Peter paused for a moment then said, "The singer, Cliff Richard. We're filming *The Young Ones* in a couple of weeks' time and I wanted to get him up to speed with the routine."

So, a few days later I met Cliff and the director of the picture, Sidney Furie, at a local gymnasium. We got on very well and Cliff was very good and picked up the routine quickly. Mr Furie was happy, and I went home having done a job well done.

A week later Peter Diamond catches up with me again and says, "You know the Cliff Richard fight?" I nodded. "Well the guy I had ready to do the fight with Cliff on the film isn't available... will you do it?" I took a moment and then told him I'd love to. So, I got on my Lambretta and rode down to ABC Studios where the fight was to be filmed.

Incidentally, I believe that the guy due to do the original fight was arrested a few nights earlier for breaking and entering... funny old game this business!

We did some initial set-ups with Robert Morley who was playing Cliff's dad in the film. I had to restrain him during a lengthy take in the back of a car. We then went in to film the fight. We'd worked it out in such a way that Robert and Cliff didn't have to do a great deal. They would throw me and my sidekick in this sequence, Val Musetti, all over the place and we'd react accordingly.

They were good days. I fell into the work because of my ability at judo. Nowadays stunt work is something people strive for. They want to be stuntmen when they leave school. I didn't know what one was until I was much older. My old man was an action actor who could ride a horse, do a bit of swordplay and was often roped into doing 'stunts' in film and TV, but I never really thought that one day I'd be doing this for a living.

Now that was my first official movie role. Well, apart from the occasion when my mum and dad were working on a film that required a tandem to ride over a level crossing. Dad was on the front, Mum was on the back and me, aged six, was put into a little sidecar contraption that was hooked onto the back of the bike. We bounced over the level crossing, I nearly fell out, but Mum and Dad had big smiles on their faces, so all must have gone well.

FROM STEED TO MONTE CARLO

After working with Cliff and the Shadows, Peter Diamond was very good to me and got me a job on a television show called *Sir Francis Drake* which was period costume and plenty of swordplay. Once again, I'd handled a sword with Dad who used to give me a few pointers which came in very handy as it happens. Anyway, one thing led to another and before long I got a job doing general stunt work on *The Avengers,* which at the time was a massive show. Many of the episodes were filmed live and the ratings were huge.

My first day. I turn up and I'm watching a stuntman called Mike Sheen who is doubling Patrick Macnee as Steed rehearsing the first part of a fight. He is to come down a flight of stairs, jump over the bannister onto a table, kick the vase of flowers into the face of the attacker and then go through a fight routine. "No sorry, Guv," says Mike, "it's not really my thing."

The fight arranger was Ray Austin, a lovely man who really knew his job. "Not really your thing?" Ray's tone was decidedly tricky. "Right then. Rocky can you do this?"

I'd watched Mike struggle through this for the last twenty-five minutes. I knew the routine, so I jumped up and said, "Like this, Ray?" I got to the bottom of the stairs and flipped over onto the table.

"Jolly good, Rocky. Go and get dressed, you're doubling Steed."

So, I went off into the wardrobe department where a young lady took my measurements and fitted me with Pierre Cardin suits, shirts made on Savile Row and of course the bowler hat. From that day on I became

Patrick Macnee's double on *The Avengers*... and began to think that this was really the greatest job in the world. I continued on *The Avengers* for another three years under Joe Dunne who had taken over from Ray Austin who had moved on to the US. Then I got a call from a guy called Joe Wadham who was an actor and a stuntman. "How would you like to come out with me and do six months on a movie?" That was quite a question after I'd got myself involved in a long running TV show. What about *The Avengers*?

Paul Weston who is now a stuntman, coordinator and second-unit director was my understudy on that show. So, he slipped on the handmade suits while I went off to colder climates.

The movie was *Monte Carlo or Bust* and it would involve some of the hairiest moments I've ever been involved with on film.

I would be doubling for Peter Cook and Joe Wadham would be doubling for Dudley Moore. One thing I will never forget was the sight of the mountain range. As I looked behind me I saw a mountain, at the bottom of the mountain was a lake and at the other side of the lake was another mountain. A span of nearly a thousand metres. They had a crane on top of one mountain and another on the opposite mountain. Each with a cable being stretched across the gap and ultimately attaching themselves to the back of my car with a quick-release system.

The car was to drive down the mountain and onto the frozen ice. The cables were attached as nobody knew if the ice was thick enough to hold the weight of the car. Nowadays technology has moved on and equipment is available that tells you within a quarter of an inch how thick the ice is... not in 1968 though.

So, Alan Parker, one of the special effects guys came to me and said, "Right this is what's going to happen. You drive down the mountain, onto the ice, if you don't crash through into the water we'll hit the quick release and you floor the gas and drive off. But if you do crash through, we can pull you out." Which was very comforting. In my opinion it's one of my finest hours. That film was such fun to work on, but what a challenge. Driving a car down the Cresta Run was something you could only see in a movie and I did it.

I drive down and crash through an ice wall, turn left and land on the Cresta Run. Now as it turned out I was pretty safe and sound inside the car. I had control of the brakes and we had spikes in the tyres, but I had to chase six blokes in an old wooden toboggan. My fear wasn't for my safety, but for them. When I took the turns, I was hitting the wall, but when they hit the walls they could quite easily have been thrown out onto the ice and I would have driven right over the poor bastards.

So, we chase four and a half miles down the mountain, two helicopters and six cameras covering it from every possible angle. My old mate Dinny Powell was quite concerned about this particular sequence and positioned himself part way down the course. "I'll be waiting for you, Rocky, and if anything happens I'll run in and get you out... don't you worry about anything, okay?" When he caught up with me at the finish area... some time later, he was knackered. He'd been trying to run through the snow, which in places was waist deep. It's good to have mates like that around with you on jobs like these.

The director Ken Annakin came up to me at the end of the day's shooting and told me it was, without question, the most exciting sequence he had ever filmed. I got back to my hotel room and found a case of Dom Pérignon champagne and a note from Ken telling me not to come back for the next two days.

That reminds me of a funny story about Dinny that happened whilst we were filming. We'd travelled about quite a bit visiting numerous locations and me and Dinny would always share a room. We stopped at a place one night and we were given a suite, but, in this hotel, you had to go through one room to get to the other.

I was going out with the producer's secretary at the time and we had a lovely little love affair. On this occasion Dinny had to get an early flight the following morning at five a.m. I had a day off and was going to take this young lady out. So, he says to me, "Rock, please remember that I have to get up early so when you come in tonight just keep the noise down, would you?" I let him know that everything would be fine. He went off to bed and me and the lady friend went out.

We had a nice meal, few bottles of wine, a cocktail or two and wandered back to the hotel about two a.m. We crept into the room, the door slipped out of my hand and banged against the other door, but we got away with it. Slipped into bed and had a little kiss and a cuddle. One thing led to another and a few minutes later, in the heat of passion, she starts screaming, "Rocky, Rocky, tell me you love me... please, Rocky, tell me you love me."

Just then the door crashed open and Dinny is standing in the doorway shouting, "FOR FUCK SAKE TELL HER YOU LOVE HER!!"

THANK GAWD FOR GRADE

I have to say that, after going through my life and checking back on how I got to be where I am today, I've discovered that Sir Lew Grade was a big part of it. His company, ITC, were behind many of the shows I was involved in as a jobbing stuntman: *The Champions, Randall and Hopkirk (Deceased), Department S* and its spin-off *Jason King, The Avengers* and *The Saint.*

All of these shows were filmed at Elstree Studios, so I could finish one job on *The Champions* and then go over and do a *Saint*. Primarily I was on a contract with *The Avengers*. I was Patrick Macnee's lead double. So anything else I was asked to do had to be worked around *Avengers* shooting scheduales, but what a time I had. And what an education. I was in with great stunt guys like Joe Dunne, Frank Maher, Ray Austin and Bill Sawyer who would throw me in all sorts of situations. You learn quickly when the pressure is on. Then I'd get a call from Les Crawford who was Roger Moore's lead stuntman on *The Saint*. Les was a lovely guy, but sometimes the schedule on that show was so complicated that Les would be doing action out in Black Park somewhere and back at the studio they were trying to do a fight scene. [Author's note: Black Park is a piece of ground and woodland near to Pinewood Studios, and many scenes you thought were set in expensive and exotic locations were in fact filmed there, all these years.]

So Les would call me and if I was free I'd go in and double Roger. I was always being thrown over sofas as I remember. Maybe Les didn't like being thrown over sofas! One of my claims to fame on *The Saint* is in the opening titles. Every time you see Roger throw someone over his shoulder... he's throwing me. The legsweep? Yeah, he's sweeping my legs and throwing me to the ground. Then the hand reaches out and goes to grab the gun, but it is stood on by Roger's foot... yep, it's my hand.

The four of us, Roger, Les Crawford, Patrick Macnee and me would, when we had the time, have some lunch together and drink... yes, you guessed it. Doubles! Roger's idea obviously.

The Champions was another cracking show to work on. I was Stuart Damon's double. He played Craig Stirling and alongside him Alexandra Bastedo and William Guant would use their extrasensory powers to fight world crime. Bill Sawyer would get me involved in some fight or other and, because of the characters' special powers, some of the fights look very odd indeed. Remember these days if your superpower is strength you would either CGI someone flying through the air after the punch or being thrown, or attach them to wires. We didn't have those back in 1968, so we relied on brute strength and a little trampoline.

Randall and Hopkirk, for anyone who hasn't seen the show, is fairly simple to explain. Randall and Hopkirk are a detective agency. Usual line of work: affairs, small crime. One day Marty Hopkirk leaves the office and is run down and killed by a car in the street. Jeff Randall and Marty's wife are understandably distraught. Then one-night Marty Hopkirk appears to Jeff Randall and talks to him. Not only can Jeff see him and hear him, but Marty can hear Jeff too. The crime fighting continues with hilarious consequences.

I doubled for actor Mike Pratt who played Jeff Randall on the show. He was not just an actor but a musician and lyricist too. He wrote a bunch of hits for Tommy Steele back in the day and picked up an Ivor Novello for his songwriting skills along the way.

I'd do all the fights and the long-shot stuff. At one time I was doubling him and the guy he was fighting. Budgets were small. Paul Weston used to double Kenneth Cope who played Marty Hopkirk. I was with Mike one day and he wasn't feeling his best. A bit of a session the night before had taken its toll on Mike and so he struggled on, but most of the scenes that day were fight orientated, so I got to cover for him. He was to be taken home in a car and was so tired that he climbed into the back seat and threw a blanket over himself and nodded off. The driver got in and drove away. The following day Mike was late to set. We assumed he was at home still feeling worse for wear. He turns up about an hour or so later. I asked him what had happened. "I'd fallen asleep in the car, I don't know how long for, but when I woke up we'd stopped at a petrol station. I thought I'd pop in and have a pee before we set off again. Well, when I came out the car had gone. Took me forty-five minutes to get a cab and then I had to walk the last part of the way as the council had closed part of the road." Turned out that when Mike had nipped in to the petrol station toilets he'd thrown the blanket onto the back seat. The driver had returned, had a look in the back, assumed that Mike was under that blanket somewhere and driven off.

So, as I said, Sir Lew Grade is responsible for a great deal of my early work. The stunt coordinators too, obviously, but it's nice to know that a great many of the top-rated shows during the sixties and seventies were made or produced by ITC.

SEAN, ROGER AND THIRTEEN MISS WORLDS

Pinewood Studios is the home of the British film industry. I've been lucky enough to be in and around the place for many of my fifty-plus years in the business. I've met many wonderful people and many who are still my dear friends. Roger Moore is known the world over as James Bond. I knew him first on the television series *The Saint* which I'd worked on with his stunt double, Les Crawford. In those days fights were the bread and butter of a jobbing stuntman. I'd worked on *The Avengers* so knew a thing or two about throwing punches and Les was another first-class punch thrower, but when it comes to a who's best list Roger Moore is right up there. When he throws a punch on screen, he means it even though he is the sweetest man you could want to meet. I've had many a good on-screen bust-up with Roger.

Anyway, one day me and Les are having lunch at the studio and we are walking back when from a side corridor we see Roger who shouts, "Rocky, Leslie, come here quick!"

We go off down the corridor and he pulls us both around the corner. Me and Les look at each other, then Roger, and say in unison, "What?"

Roger, a master of comedic timing, looks up and down the corridor then leans into us and whispers, "You're looking at the new James Bond." Well we couldn't believe it. We started cheering and whooping. He told us to shut up and took us into his dressing room. "Here you are, lads. Let's celebrate, eh?" He produced a bottle of champagne and we drank in his good news. Great news for Les too as he was Roger's chief stuntman at this time and would most certainly get the job of doubling him on the Bonds.

I'd started my Bond connection back at the start with Sean Connery on *From Russia with Love*. Mostly fights, but a great way to make a living back then for a young up-and-coming performer. Bob Simmons and Peter Perkins who were the stunt arrangers had realized that the action sequences in these films were so big that they needed to find as many performers to work in the one place at one time. My dad had done a few days and I got a call to go down, too. Just background stuff really, Peter Diamond doing high falls from the walls of this set and Fred Haggerty, who had an acting role in the film, doing another. Twenty or thirty of us just slugged it out as soon as we heard, "Action!" Sean was just getting into his role of Bond during that picture and still needed brushing up on a screen fight. He clocked one or two of us during the shoot, but he was a great pupil. Bob would take him to one side and show him how this punch should work and then he would throw a world-class screen punch. As with any fight for the big screen, every punch has to be sold. Connery can certainly sell a punch.

I had a very busy mid-sixties with Bond. I started on *Casino Royale* in 1966 taking part in the casino fight sequence at the end of the movie. Terry Yorke was the stunt coordinator and was a really nice bloke. He looked after me and gave me twelve weeks' work. Now I was a young man. Twelve weeks' work at twenty-five pounds a day, cash, was a king's ransom in those days and I would come home and stuff it into a drawer in my room. The film ran into a lot of financial issues and they had a few issues with Peter Sellers and the array of directors employed to make the film. For me it was very lucrative as I'd film that during the day and go off and do *Dirty Dozen* in the evening. Then came *You Only Live Twice* which was a huge production. The massive volcano set at Pinewood was the biggest I'd ever seen, and the stunt boys were crawling about in the roof space at the entrance to the volcano dressed as ninjas. Now, I'm not the best man with ropes, but as a young man I had a do-anything with attitude. Bob Simmons had asked me to join them and slide down the ropes firing a gun at the same time. Some of the lads got themselves in bother when they didn't slow down the rope using a section of rubber tube and hit the ground, breaking an ankle. I wanted no part of that as that would mean I'd be out of work. So, I practised with the tube which, incidentally, Vic Armstrong had been asked to source for the film, and managed to get the job done. Vic is easy to spot as he is the first ninja down the ropes – I haven't a clue which one is me, but I'm there and, luckily, I have no battle scars unlike some of the other lads.

After Roger had announced his arrival as Bond to me and Les Crawford, we both got a call to work on *The Man with the Golden Gun*. I was not only a stuntman on the film but took the role of Ahmed who along with Terry Plummer tries to beat up Bond in Beirut as he is entertaining a belly dancer. Now, as with many of the occasions I've worked with Roger, there is always a funny story.

The night before I'd been out and got a bit drunk with my mates. I got in late and had received a phone call to say I was required on set the following morning. Well, I was not in a fit state to go to work, but it's a Bond movie and you don't turn them down. So, I rushed off to bed to get some sleep. Get to Pinewood in the morning and have time for a shower and shave. Get to set as Ahmed and Les Crawford is coordinating. We go through the fight and Roger has been told that I'm a bit worse for wear so, when it comes to the part of the fight where he bashes my head against the wall I can hear him saying, "Sorry Rocky, sorry Rocky, sorry Rocky…" A lovely man and I got the chance to do it all over again next time around on *The Spy Who Loved Me*.

[Author's note: during that fight sequence in *The Man with The Golden Gun* a mirror on the wall moved and you can see the camera crew filming the fight on the stage. At the time and with the technology we had then it was impossible to see this error in continuity, but nowadays you can see everything. In some cuts of the movie the error has been removed entirely.]

I thought the volcano sequence was big, but this set on the brand new '007 Stage' was beyond belief. A flooded set that housed nuclear submarines and a fight to the death between us boys in red and that lot in blue. I was lucky again as I knew Bob Simmons quite well and would often pick him up from his home in Ealing and drive him into work. Bob didn't drive after his drinking got a bit much and so I became his taxi.

Ironically on the strength of this gesture he would repay me with a job here and there. *The Spy Who Loved Me* was one such outing. I was involved in a couple of set pieces including detaining the lovely leading lady, Barbara Bach, while Roger was being held by Jimmy Lodge; and the overturning of the yellow Mini Moke which was blown up, with me at the wheel, Jimmy Lodge next to me and Paul Weston bailing out before we hit the water. It was six great weeks on one of Roger's best outings as 007.

My next Bond job was on *For Your Eyes Only*. I was only on it for a few days, but it was a crucial part of the movie. I was a crew member aboard the *St Georges* which was a fishing boat being used by the Navy to monitor the Russians. We had a stage where tip tanks were built next to the ship and, as the explosions go off when a stray World War Two mine hits the side of the ship, I get thrown from one side to the other whilst being drowned by the huge wave of water. An unusual job, but good to see on screen when it's all edited together. I also remember a punch-up on the deck of a ship on that picture. Roger and Topol arrive in Albania and their crew start to fight the villain's henchmen. A good punch-up, but only a few days' work. Roger and Topol got on really well. They were like a double act for a while. Someone would come up to Topol and say, "I loved *Fiddler on the Roof*, and he would say, "If I had a nickel for every time someone said that to me." From behind him Roger would sing, "You would be a rich man."

Roger came back in *Octopussy* and so did I. Not only working at Pinewood, but in a sensational trip to India as Roger's double. I turned up in India and was expecting to check into my hotel with the rest of the stunt boys. Roger and the cast were in the Shiv Niwas hotel and I was to stay in the Lake Palace hotel. "Now, Rocky, you're doubling Roger, yes?" This was one of the location assistants who was sorting out accommodation.

"Yes, that's right, now which room am I in?"

He looked down his list and said, "Right, it's like this. We're going to put you in with the thirteen Miss Worlds. Now are you okay with that? I can move you if you like." Bless him he was asking me if it was okay to be in a hotel with thirteen Miss Worlds who were playing Octopussy's girls in the film. What a way to make a living. A rumour had been circulated that a man had infiltrated the hotel with the Miss Worlds and was paying each of them a visit during the night… I would love to say that I had something to do with this, but alas I was otherwise engaged. But then James Bond allows certain doors to be opened for you. I mean, where else would you get thirteen Miss Worlds in one movie?

While I was in India we heard of Martin Grace's accident filming the train sequence in Peterborough. Martin had been Roger's chief stuntman since *The Spy Who Loved Me* and was a very competent and professional performer. The sequence called for Martin to be hanging on the side of the train carrying Octopussy and her circus to its next show. Bond is being chased by the villain. All had been going well. Arthur Wooster was directing the second unit from a helicopter following the train. A shot needed to be redone and, instead of the train returning to its number one position, they carried on filming along a section of track that hadn't been cleared as safe. Martin struck a concrete post on the side of the track which threw him up into the air, breaking his pelvis. He held on by his fingertips until the train came to a standstill. I was asked to fly back and take over where Martin left off.

When I got back to the UK things had changed a bit and now Paul Weston was doubling Roger along with Jim Dowdall so my involvement in the train sequence was cut way back, but I did double Roger after he is thrown from the train. Wearing the Bond wig, I had to forward roll down an embankment and run through the undergrowth. It wasn't much but I made Roger look good, and that's all that mattered.

Whilst I was on *Octopussy* I received a call from Vic Armstrong who was working with Sean Connery on his return to the world of Bond in *Never Say Never Again*. Not only did I get to double Sean in the opening sequence running through the undergrowth, but I then got strangled by Sean as he attacked the building, and had a fight with him as he tried to save Vic's wife and stuntwoman, Wendy Leech, who then stabbed him… women eh?

My most recent outing with Bond was in *Skyfall*. Daniel Craig was Bond and Gary Powell now stunt coordinator. Gary really does do a great job on the new Bonds and it was a joy to be involved in the London sequences. As it was the fiftieth anniversary Gary had brought together as many stunt performers who had worked on previous Bonds to work and get a credit on this one.

Bond is running down Whitehall and the traffic comes to a standstill as he runs down the middle of the road. I was in one of those cars. I didn't flip it over or blow it up, I just sat there and watched Daniel Craig run by. Daniel is a nice guy and a very fine actor. We met him during the safety briefing. This happens before every set-up, often due to gunfire going off, but in this instance, traffic would be driving past the leading man. This driving job could have been done by anyone. But Gary puts stunt people in just in case there is the slightest possibility of a risk. If Gary had asked me to slide a car or turn one over I'd have jumped at the chance, but because it's a Bond I'd have done anything. They are very special to me. Now I ask you who'd turn down a few days' work doing that? Exactly.

EVERYONE'S A WINNER BABY

EXCEPT MICHAEL

June 1985 started as any other. I had been working solidly during that year having finished *My Beautiful Launderette, Spies Like Us* and the new Biggles movie. Marc Boyle had been given the job of coordinating the action on the latest instalment of the *Death Wish* franchise directed by Michael Winner. It was to be filmed in London and the streets were to be turned into battle-scarred New York tenements as gang warfare ensued. I was one of a big team brought in to take part in the action. I'd done a fair bit of work on the picture, including motorbike falls and fights, but my big part in this film would be a fall from a burning building.

Marc took me up to the roof to show me where the fire was to be and, more importantly, where I was to be. I could see the landing area and I had an escape route at the back of the roof, a set of stairs, should I need to use them. All was good. I was to come back later that day for the take.

Marc was a nice guy, a good stuntman who I'd worked with on many shows in the past including *The Sweeney* and *The Professionals*. He'd been coordinating for years and had always looked after his stunt guys and girls. He walked me through everything step by step, making everything very clear that if there was a problem I'd have a plan B, a luxury that many stunt guys hadn't had in the past. Marc wanted to put himself in the performer's place, because he'd done the job before and knew the type of problems that could arise.

Now as a stuntman you have to have a good working relationship with the special effects crew. The two teams work hand in hand and the relationship is very much based on trust. You as the stuntman trust the special effects man to have put the right amount of gunpowder in this charge, so you don't get your head blown off as the camera rolls.

What had happened between the rehearsal and the take was pretty obvious for all to see. Mr Winner had approached the special effects man and asked for more explosions, much bigger than anticipated. Michael Winner could be a formidable character. He had a reputation for getting what he wanted and certain members of the crew were a bit frightened of him. So, when he says he wants more fire and a bigger explosion, he expects it. However, let's analyze that for a second. Can anyone see how dangerous this attitude is? Of course you can. It doesn't take a degree at a world-famous university to tell you that if you overlook the very obvious safety aspects of a stunt like this, people will get injured. Yes, you want the audience to gasp and say how amazing that scene was, but at what cost? A life? When you work with petrol, or fuel of any kind, you work with limited quantities, so you remain in control. Nowadays much of the fire you see on screen can be CGI and put on afterwards, but some will still be required on set during filming. This will be controlled by gas. The special effects team can pump gas into the fire to increase the size of the flames and turn it down in between takes. This gives the impression that this fire is raging out of control.

This was a different scenario for me as the building I was to jump from was to be demolished at the end of the sequence. No chance of a second take here. So, everything had to be spot on.

What hadn't been factored in was the director's involvement in this. The fuel tanks were lashed together inside the building and would explode causing huge amounts of destruction.

I got up onto the roof and got to my start position. I could smell petrol. You know the way you drive onto the forecourt of a petrol station? You get out of your car, walk to the pump and you can smell fuel. Well it was like that only stronger. I heard the assistant director giving the cue for the cameramen for "light the building," then "roll cameras" then I heard "Action!" The building went up so fast, too fast for me to get through my routine. I heard this deafening WOOOOOSH as the flames engulfed everything. My heart was pounding out of my chest. I was trying to take short breaths to prevent me from breathing in the thick black smoke that was suddenly all around me. The flames were fifteen feet high in front of me and all around me. I thought *Fuck this for a game of soldiers, I need to get out of here and fast.* I turned to go for the stairs, but they'd gone. The escape route that Marc had told me about had vanished. Crumbled clean away.

It was at that moment that I had what people now refer to as 'complete recollection'. My family, my life, my friends, faces, places all rushing by me, filling up my head, preparing me for my ultimate doom which I suspected was only moments away. So, this is how it was going to end, eh? Me been done up like a kipper at the top of this building? Not bloody likely! I had to find a way down.

The building was falling apart around me. Intense heat forced me further and further away from the edge of the building. I had to make a split-second decision. Do I jump and hope for the best or stay here and burn to death? Jumping was the best choice out of the two, but I couldn't see the box rig. It was there somewhere, to the left a bit more I think, but where? I was going to have to take a leap of faith. You hear about these decisions, but you never think you'll have to make one, particularly on something as clinical as a film set. The heat was intense, I could feel my skin burning, if I waited much longer I wouldn't be able to jump at all. Easy choice for me. I picked a spot and jumped. I put my hands up to my face to protect my eyes from the flames. A moment of silence. I heard nothing, no sound at all. A total deafness, which in hindsight was quite a comfort. I would have expected to hear a rushing of the breeze or the crackling of the flames, but nothing. I took my hands away from my face. I opened my eyes and saw the landing rig but was never going to hit it. I was just too far to the left to make a good landing, or should I say a poor landing better than it eventually turned out. This is when the slo-mo kicked in. I'd come through the smoke and flames and now I was watching the box rig approaching. I was going to hit it, but it wasn't going to be pretty. In fact, in those last seconds of the fall I prepared myself for the worst.

I assumed that I'd be thrown to my left, bang my head and that would be it... lights out; but I landed feet first, one leg on and one off. A piercing pain raced through me, like I'd been shot. I've never been shot but shooting victims do refer to this sharp shooting pain. I screamed out and nearly passed out. My lungs filled with smoke and I blew as much of it out as I could with that scream. I screamed till I had nothing left, my vision went blurry and I was about to pass out.

My stunt colleague, Jazzer Jeyes, was first on scene. He'd jumped from a lower floor and watched my fall. I couldn't feel my legs, my back was broken, my pelvis had snapped, and I thought I was going to die. As far as I was concerned this was to be my last day. It would have been too if it wasn't for the actions of the on-set ambulance crew who made me as stable as they could before being transferred to an ambulance for the journey to hospital.

I was taken to St Thomas' Hospital, convenient as we were filming in the old hospital complex. Luckily for me Doctor Radford was phoned at home and informed of the accident and was asked to come in. My face and hands were burnt, the smell of burning flesh lingered in the room and that isn't something that you can move on from. It stays with you. I was in the corridor and my daughter turned up and was so shocked with what she had seen she was physically sick. They took me up to a room, I had tubes in and out of everywhere and I mean everywhere. Doctor Radford came up, examined me and said, "Do you still want to do stunt work?"

Not the first question I'd expected, but under the circumstances it seemed fair. "Why?" I said with what little voice I had left.

He continued, "Because if you do I'm going to have to operate and if you don't, well I can leave you as you are." I had to go back to work, it was my life, my livelihood. He looked at me and said in a gentle voice, "Well, in that case I'll be seeing you very soon."

That is where all the operations began. I had a five-inch difference on my left side caused by the impact with the ground, so a metal pin was drilled into my knee and weights were attached. In turn this was set outside the bed so, each day, a further weight was added and slowly the left side would return to its original position. Only when this stage was complete could I have another operation where a metal frame was placed inside my pelvis. Scaffolding if you like, to support the bones and aid the healing. This, it turns out, is the reason why today I have no limp.

Added to this my other internal injuries had to be treated and fixed. It took many operations to move my intestines back into place, removing damaged sections and stitching up the new joins. My testicles had to be realigned as they had been damaged in the impact. This was not a simple procedure and consequently has caused me many years of physical and mental trauma. For the next seven weeks I lay in my hospital bed and stared at the ceiling, being moved once a day, by only an inch, one way and then back.

I was on morphine for the pain which I highly recommend. The television was on one day and as the morphine kicked in the pain left me and I became aware of open spaces, green grass, the wind in my hair and a man on my back! I realized that my perspective of my surroundings had changed, and I was unable to put my finger on what was going on. Then it hit me! "I'm a horse!" Yes, my watching the racing on the television had caused me to take flight as a horse. Great stuff and an endorsement for all morphine users the world over... well, not all but you know what I mean. I couldn't have been without it.

This time I spent in hospital was a major moment in my life and, as you've already found out, for a great deal of that time I was under heavy sedation. I recently uncovered a medical report from St Thomas' Hospital which gave a detailed breakdown of my condition upon arrival and my initial progress and their findings. Here is some of that report:

'Mr Taylor arrived at 17.10hrs in a moderately shocked and burnt condition. His pulse rate on arrival was 120 per minute; blood pressure 100m.m/50 m.m and his respirations were 48 per minute. His face was covered in fairly superficial burns and his most serious injury was to the pelvis, which clinically and radiologically had sustained a severe disruption.

'The left hemi-pelvis had been forced upwards (proximally) by a distance of approximately 2" as a result of the impact of the extended leg with the ground. Fractures had occurred in the left wing of the ilium

close to the sacroiliac joint and the pubic symphysis joint had been disrupted. There was also a fracture of the left L.5 lumbar transverse process. There were no other fractures.

'1ˢᵗ Operating session 19.6.85: Cystoscopy was performed; this showed the inside of the bladder to be substantially intact and the small retroperitoneal tear was not seen. A catheter was passed without difficulty.

'A traction pin was then inserted into the left tibia, so the pelvic fracture could be temporarily stabilized by skeletal traction.

'The surgeon in charge of the fixation of the severely displaced pelvic fracture would be Mr David Reynolds.

'Major pelvic reconstructive surgery is not widely practised in this country, but we felt there was no possibility of Mr Taylor ever returning to his work as a stuntman without an accurate reassembly of his pelvis. The operation was not without risk and careful planning was necessary.

'In the event the procedure, which was performed on 27.6.85, went entirely according to plan and two large threaded rods were inserted posteriorly across the pelvis and through a separate incision anteriorly two substantial plates were bolted into the pelvis at the pubic symphysis.

'Following the operation Mr Taylor's condition improved progressively after a very difficult first few post-operative days.

'The records show that a total of 18 units of blood were cross matched for Mr Taylor, of which 13 were given during his stay. He was discharged on 17ᵗʰ July 1985, walking on crutches with arrangements for outpatient follow-up.'

My girlfriend at the time was Marlene who I just couldn't have been without. She came to visit all the time, brought me soup and never missed a single day. My mother would often come up to see me too. It's an extraordinary thing the way people's lives are brought together through tragedy, isn't it? I had been moved from one ward to a private room, primarily because I was screaming out in pain the whole time. When I woke up one day the wall of my room was covered from top to bottom with cards from friends, family and everyday people like you who had seen the news footage of my accident and written a card sending me best wishes. I was moved to tears and to this day I still get a lump in my throat when I think of the thousands of people who cared enough to do this simple gesture. It meant so much. I never got chance at the time to say it so "Thank you so very much."

One of my fellow stunt performers on that picture was Gareth Milne. A fine stuntman and good pal. These are his words. He remembers what happened on that day.

'During my forty-year career as a stuntman it has been my misfortune to be present at a fair few horrendous, on-set accidents. They all have one thing in common and that is that none of them should have happened.

'In the big picture however, these instances are rare, and the professionalism of the stunt people involved in our industry has prevailed to ensure that the safety aspects are adhered to and guidelines evolved from many years of experience are followed.

'To categorize these accidents I would say that the majority were caused by either honest or dishonest miscalculation on behalf of the production or coordinator, lack of resources or equipment failure of one kind or another.

'Rocky's accident was different. It was caused by one man's ego, ignorance and inability to leave anything to the experts who were employed to ensure a safe outcome.

'The memories of the day are still fairly clear but after all these years it still resounds with me and, to my surprise, I found myself getting angry all over again.

'It was a bright day, warm with a moderate wind. We arrived on set early as usual and by the time we had gone through the works of costume and make-up we were called directly to set. A building with a flat roof had been fabricated out of scaffolding and clad with ply. It stood about 35ft high, had windows but was hollow inside to accommodate a "Dante". This is a special effects device which spews burning diesel or similar accelerant in all directions. I remember it being quite a large affair. Not something you would want to get too close to when it was a light and working.

'I was not party to discussions nor do I know whether the idea of seeing a man on the roof of this burning building had been discussed

34

prior to the day. Usually any similar stunt would have been done with gas, so the effects operatives have control over the intensity of the burn and can turn the whole thing off if there was a problem. I remember the Effects supervisor expressing his opinion that his brief had been to burn the building full stop and that once the Dante was working then the building would in his words "Really go."

'While this was ongoing a JCB was in the process of digging a large pit outside one wall of the building which was to house a catching box rig as the man on the roof would be required to jump off in shot. The man in question was Rocky Taylor.

'Myself and the assembled stunt team were starting to get anxious at these developments and asked for an escape route in the form of a large extension ladder to be erected on the off-camera wall of the building which was done at the last minute. We also inspected the roof and jump-off point. The finished pit now containing the box rig looked adequate, but you would have had to have had a good view of it and spotted your landing point before committing to the jump. Also, an old burnt-out car had been placed very near to the far lip of the pit for what reason I still am not sure.

'This had now become an overly complicated and quite dangerous situation but still manageable had Rocky been able to take his own timing for the jump i.e. before his vision was obscured by flames or it got too hot.

'Enter Michael Winner. I will not stoop to trying to describe his personality as better writers have tried and, in my opinion, not quite come up to the mark.

'He had a tower built for himself on which he alone stood with a loudhailer in one hand and his cigar in the other surveying his assembled minions with the gimlet eyes of a market trader sneering and berating us with unprintable expletives.

'We of the stunt crew were all whispering to each other that at least someone must have given him a cueing system to give Rocky the benefit of taking his own time for the jump. This would have gone thus. First cue would be to roll cameras then to bring up the flames slowly. Rocky would then take his own cue.

'Whether anyone did or not, Winner was going to do this his way.

'"Start the fire!" he screamed through the bullhorn. Immediately we knew there was a large problem brewing. As the flames began to emit from the building, "More flame. More flame!" he screeched. The flame duly obliged. The camera crews watched open mouthed still waiting their cue to roll. A few shouted, "Go Rocky. Get out of there!" Our hearts were in our mouths as the fire completely consumed the building and Rocky was still on the roof.

'I and a few of the team broke ranks and ran to where we had put the escape ladder. We could not get within ten feet of the base of it.

'That's when we heard it. A loud sickening thud from the catching rig side of the building. Rocky had waited as long as he could for the roll-camera cue that never came. Burnt and blinded he could not spot his landing, overshot and landed half in the rig and half on the old car placed close by it.

'I accompanied him to hospital in the ambulance. He was conscious. He knew how much damage he had done to his body and was incredulous at how he had been hung out to dry by circumstances largely out of his control.

'I took a taxi back to the set after a couple of hours with him. They had wrapped, and everyone had gone home. The burning building had been extinguished and was a complete blackened, twisted shell. Only Michael Winner's tower still stood.'

Gareth Milne February 2018

Marlene was my partner at the time and she recalls that period from her point of view:

'Rocky and I went out together for many years until life-changing events occurred on the day of the accident.

'I was viewing houses in Chiswick that day and had just walked back into the house when the phone rang. It was Rocky's daughter Simone who blurted out, "Dad's had an accident on set, he's been taken to St Thomas' Hospital. Marlena, it's serious."

'Rocky was working on Death Wish III, *with Charles Bronson and was playing a thug. I rushed from Chiswick to the hospital to meet Julie and Simone in the lobby. The doctor advised us that Rocky was very very*

sick and had been badly burnt and injured following the fall. He was just off to surgery to perform the first operation in the UK of implanting metal plates onto the pelvic bone to mend the structure. Rocky also had a burst bladder, ruptured bowel, severe burns and was so swollen from the impact with the boxes that were there to prevent injury. We were told that if he pulled through this he'd be the luckiest man alive.

'I said to the girls, "Let's go in and no matter what Dad looks like, let's pretend that he looks fine and all is okay. We must bolster him up, give him hope and confidence." So, in we went. Julie had one hand and Simone had the other. They dug their nails in so deeply into my hands as we tried to talk to Rocky. He was already prepped for surgery and was slurring his words. When we left the room the girls both burst into tears. It was quite an emotional night. Rocky was in surgery for five hours. We were told to go home. The next day, I went to the hospital. Rocky was heavily sedated, his burns and his face swathed in ointment and gauze. Days went by and gradually he opened his eyes and returned to us all. I brought in healthy food on a daily basis and fed it to him, I read to him and we watched Boris Becker win Wimbledon for the first time.

'Then one day, the door swung open and there stood Michael Winner with a photo journalist by his side. "Hello love," he wailed, "I've got some papers for you to sign." Meanwhile the photographer was taking photo after photo of Rocky, telling him to put his thumbs up in the air to signify he was on the mend! It was dreadful. I cut in, "Rocky will not be signing any of your paperwork, he is in no position to do so." Winner looked up at me from his glasses. "It's none of your bloody business!" he shouted across at me. I was trying to remain calm, but if he thought that I was just going to sit here and take that from him, he had another thing coming! "Oh yes, it is my business. I'm taking care of all Rocky's affairs and he will not be signing any paper work. Do you understand me, Winner?" I was very angry by this time. As far as I was concerned he didn't deserve to be called by his first name any more and I dropped the mister as well.

'The papers he was referring to exonerated Cannon Films of all wrong doing and prevented Rocky from seeking legal representation for the accident and injuries he suffered. Winner strode around the bed

37

exclaiming, "If Rocky doesn't sign these papers then I can promise you he will never work in the film business again," and he finished with, "If he doesn't sign, it will take him five years before his case comes to court and we will fight him every step of the way." I was already chomping at the bit to scream my reply back to him, "He's not signing, and that's an end of it. Now get out, oh and goodbye Mr Winner!" With that he flounced off angrily clutching a small fluffy, toy gorilla in his hands with the journalist trailing behind.

'Rocky was in hospital for just over two months. I visited from nine a.m. till nine p.m. every day as it seemed to boost his general outlook on life. He seemed to like having me around. This gave him a sense of normality. He was treated with the strongest painkillers and the burns on his face and hands took months to heal, leaving marks on his face and hands where he had tried to shield his face from the flames. When he was released from hospital, he was incontinent, could not walk, his skin was badly burnt from the fire and he kept getting the most terrifying panic attacks and flashbacks.

'It was wonderful how people rallied around to help Rocky after the accident. Cubby Broccoli sent a hamper from Fortnum and Mason, Robert Wagner sent £500, Michael Caine would call at the house and many other big stars would send cards and gifts to the house. I created a lovely scrapbook containing all of the wonderful cards and letters he'd received. A benefit was held at Pinewood Studios and had been organized by his wonderful stunt colleagues. Rocky later appeared on Breakfast TV *and on various other TV and radio shows to talk about the accident.*

'Rocky came home to Chiswick, which with two flights of stairs wasn't ideal for him. Initially he had a nurse visit on a daily basis but for some reason these visits stopped, and I looked after Rocky full time. It was quite a battle for Rocky, having been a very able-bodied man, he was suddenly bed-/settee-ridden and kept getting panic attacks, couldn't walk and had severe problems with his waterworks. I would cradle him in my arms and comfort him through these frightening attacks. Slowly, he learned to walk again. I took him to physiotherapy on a daily basis where he swam and attempted to walk on machines. When he was at

home I would insist that he took an extra step every day on our little walks. Sometimes the tears would roll down his face, as he was trying to go on and didn't want to let me down. It was a dreadful time and we were living off my earnings as a model and film extra, but that was infrequent as I really didn't like to leave him on his own for too long. The stunt boys would visit him and cheer him up which boosted his morale, but sadly he was frustrated and angry at his condition and his mood would worsen and cause him to erupt over the smallest thing. One time, it took its toll on me and I told him that it would be best, for us both, if we went our separate ways so he could be at home with his daughters. He was able to walk by then and was very much on the mend. We have always stayed friends throughout and five years later, as predicted by Michael Winner, we had our court date fixed and duly made our way to the courts for the case against Cannon films for breach of his safety.

'It had been recorded by Thames Television, on that fateful day. Michael Winner was recorded as saying, "Turn up the flames, turn up the bloody flames!" Poor Rocky was up on the roof, not wearing a fire suit and before he could realize what was going on, the whole building was on fire and Rocky had to jump blind through the flames and to safety. Sadly, missing the boxes and crashing to earth hitting the ground very hard indeed.

'On the morning of the case Rocky was approached by Cannon Films and offered a settlement fee. After some time had gone by Rocky accepted a figure, which considering what he had been through was never going to be enough for the lifetime of injuries and the years of misery. Rocky Taylor had worked his way to the very top of his profession only to have all those years of dedication and determination thrown away by Michael Winner's irresponsible, devil may care attitude towards another human being."'

My daughter Simone remembers a more personal side to the events. Firstly, about how she heard the news.

"I remember being on the phone to Nan reading a letter from Julie in South Africa when the operator interrupted our phone call saying they had a very urgent call trying to get through. Suddenly Greg Powell was on the phone telling me you had been involved in a serious accident and

that Nosher (Powell – Greg's dad) was on his way to get me. Poor man was still on the line and nearly had a heart attack! It seemed like forever but in a very short time Nosher was at home and drove me in a very short space of time, his headlights flashing and hand on the horn. I reached St Thomas' Hospital from Putney in record time! The Sun *newspaper was already there. I came to see you and Marlena, and I walked with you as far as we could to theatre. I've never prayed so hard and much in my life… I remember* The Sun *reporter send me a bouquet of flowers a few days later apologizing for their intrusion as I had been quite rude to them as they were preventing me trying to get into the hospital to get to you. I also remember you being on the 10 o'clock news that night as well and making the front pages the next day.*

'A few days later Michel Winner sent you a get-well card and paper-clipped a ten-pound note. He thought in his sick way it was funny to call it your adjustment money! Your stunt job went from a fall/jump to a full-blown fire stunt. That was like adding insult to injury. Disgusting summed him up, really.

[Author's note: an adjustment is the term for a sum of money a stunt performer receives for an additional stunt on set. So, I arrive on set and am in a fight scene. I get paid a day rate for that. Part way through the morning the stunt coordinator asks if I would do a fall from a building or be knocked down by a car. If I agree, I will receive an additional fee for this stunt on top of my daily rate.]

Lloyd Bass is a very fine stunt coordinator and performer. But back in 1985 he was a school kid watching the filming. This is how he remembers that time.

'I was living and schooling in London at the time of Death Wish III.

'Having always wanted to be a stuntman, I was intrigued to find out that they were filming in Lambeth less than 1 mile from my home. I made my way to the location only to find hordes of people crammed up against gates trying to get a peek of the filming.

'Being a child of only fourteen it wasn't difficult to make my way to the front politely asking the grown-ups to let me through.

'So, I stand for most of the day at this gate watching filming, and if I am totally honest, not really understanding what I was seeing being

that my desire to be a stuntman was mostly through watching many of the stunt filled dramas on TV.

'There were lots of people looking really aggressive, on a set that looked amazingly how my imagination had thought the Bronx might look.

'Crew and equipment everywhere, I was totally in my element. So then comes the big gag, the building fire and a man about to jump off.

'So, some time passes and of course the structure is lit, the smoke filled the skies quickly and the stuntman jumped through the smoke to the ground... unbeknown to me the stunt was not the success I had thought and all the emergency services and chaos after the jump, to me, looked normal because I had nothing to compare it to. Later of course, the news reported a different reality than the one I thought I had seen.

'Obviously by now I know the stuntman was Rocky Taylor.

'My passion for stunts didn't end with the knowledge of the accident and in fact I am now and have been a member myself of the British Stunt Register since 1999. Best of all, Rocky's was not only my first ever stunt seen performed in the flesh, but he is one of best friends now and I am humbled every time I am in his company.

'I had no idea on the day that some the other people performing stunts and running to the aid of Rocky that day, would end up being some of my esteemed colleagues and friends in the stunt business today.

'I remember the day when I finally had the opportunity to explain my story to the great Rocky Taylor, and to continue from that day with a friendship that neither of us knew, on that fateful day, would ever become one.

GETTING BACK TO WORK AIN'T EASY

When you've been laid up for any period of time, getting back into a routine is never easy. Getting back to work was something that I had assumed would be like falling off a log... no pun intended! I suddenly had limitations in my repertoire. Things that came as second nature to me were very far from my grasp. I was a knockabout stuntman back in the day. I couldn't do a stair fall again. Not with my back. I was a first-rate horseman and would never be able to pull a horse down again. Not with my back. So once the realization had kicked in that I would have to become a very different performer from the other Rocky Taylor, I could try and ease myself back without further injury.

The standard bag of tricks that I had surrounded myself with over the last twenty years had been whittled down to driving, sword play and fights. My high fall days were over, but where would I start? Well luckily, I had mates like Peter Brayham who rang me and said, "Rock, how you doing? You okay for a driving job next week on *Boon*?" I could always rely on Peter to get me out of a jam. A few days' work here, a weeks' worth there, he was consistent. Eddie Stacey found me work too. Similar work, but enough to keep my head above water for a bit longer.

I was doing lots of driving jobs during the period. Motorcycles and cars. For *The Bill* I was driving around the streets of London as either the villain or the police. For *Boon* I was on motorbike and in an acting role too. To a job on *Who Framed Roger Rabbit?* Peter Diamond was the coordinator and we go back a long way. He gave me my first job as you remember. So, I owe Peter a lot. He tells me he's working on an animated feature with Bob Hoskins and would I like to be involved? Well, I can't say no. So down I go to Borehamwood Studios to find out what is going on. As luck would have it I found myself in a very early stage of what we now call 'motion capture' work. So, whenever you see the rabbit on the screen it's animated, but whenever you see the rabbit in shadow or silhouette on a wall or window… it's me. Nowadays entire units are set up to do motion capture, but back then I was asked to stand in a poorly lit room and to hold a puppet that looked the rabbit. They lit the shape in such a way that you couldn't tell the difference. Very strange and yet very satisfying. You can see how important these puppeteers are to the *Star Wars* movies and the like from me doing my work on this. No falling down or skidding round corners for me on this one.

Having worked on many films and TV shows I do get the occasional residual payment from time to time. Lots of *Avengers* from the sixties. I was in so many episodes that they keep coming in to this day, which is lovely. I'm lucky in a way as all those shows from the sixties that I was involved in are still being screened, which means that I still get paid. Which is a lovely bonus. In particular the Harry Potter series. Now here's a funny thing. In the UK we don't get residual payments for films, only TV shows, and yet at the time of the first Harry Potter going onto production a strike had been called by the Union. Consequently, the only way the studios and film companies had agreed was to pay residual payments and had written it into our contracts. Well, we signed as we didn't expect them to do the sort of business they did. Now, every time a Harry Potter film is shown somewhere on the planet, I get paid. Now these payments are sometimes the difference between paying the mortgage or taking out a loan.

With some of the money from my compensation I bought a lease on a pub and refurbished it with my photos on all the walls and created a very show-biz atmosphere. There was a stage with a piano and we were looking for a slightly older clientele in a piano bar – wrong – it was to be one of the most successful karaoke clubs in the country. For the next nine years we ran the club and had the very best time. People came from far and wide. Gravesend and Brighton were deserted on a Friday night as everyone who was anyone came to Cobham for a night to remember.

Mark Davies was my compere and pianist. A brilliant vocalist who was sadly overlooked on *The X-Factor* otherwise it could have been a very different story for him. In fact, Steve Brookstein who won *The X-Factor* has always said that his career started in my club.

Having the nightclub meant I could use it for all the corporate film and TV parties that would go on. The stunt boys had their meetings there, first assistants and their teams would come for events. Christmas was booked a year or so in advance. Everyone who was anyone wanted to have a do at 'Rocky's', and who could blame them? It was first class entertainment, with good times for all.

I even sang for the crowds every night. They'd start chanting, "ROCKY, ROCKY, ROCKY!" I turned up on stage and Mark would play the opening chords to *Delilah* by Tom Jones. Once I was done and the night was over I still had to get them out. "All right, ladies and gentlemen, we've all had fun but it's time to go home now, go on off you go, see you again tomorrow night." You would, too. Jim Davidson and Jimmy Tarbuck opened the club for me and all my golfing pals were there – John Virgo, Dennis Waterman, Jess Conrad, Kenny Lynch, and Jimmy Capaldi – great days.

Sadly, nine years later after all the great times we'd had it was time to move on and Punch Taverns had sent builders in looking to redevelop, so they made me an offer I couldn't refuse. Such a shame. A great place, not only for me but for the community. There was a great deal of community back then. The locals loved the place and many travelled from far and wide. It really needed something to replace it. You know, for the next generation. Oh well we live in hope, eh?

Also, just as a final point about the club. You always run the risk of robbery. We had heard through the pub grapevine that a team of 'bastards' were knocking off pubs and restaurants up and down the county. We had a doorman, we had CCTV and as many mod cons as possible to try and prevent any security breach. I was away one weekend to a Henry Cooper Variety Club golf do in Newcastle when I received a phone call from the police to say we'd been broken into. Turns out that on this particular occasion a few folks had stayed behind at the end of the night for 'after's'. What we lovingly refer to as 'a drink on us'. Included were my daughter Simone and her husband Gary, one of the doormen, a great big fella, his girlfriend and Dave Dogg, a local musician. Pammy had gone to bed upstairs. She was woken at about a quarter to one by banging sounds which unnerved her. Now on this night we'd had a blues band playing downstairs and the club had its own stage area which needed to be dismantled after each gig. With me so far? Good.

She had assumed that this noise was just that. The stage being broken down. So Felicity, who worked behind the bar, had gone outside for a moment and was confronted by a gunman who forced her back inside. He took all the money from the till in the bar. Not long after this the bedroom door is flung open and another man in a ski mask holding a gun enters the room. Not only was he holding a gun, but he had a hostage, my daughter Simone, the gun pushed against her head. [Author's note: I must just say here that Simone and her husband were living nearby but, on this occasion, had agreed to stay in the club instead of going home as it made Pammy feel better having someone else there.] The robber came upstairs because the safe was upstairs. His mate had worked the room downstairs, now it was his turn and he was confronted by my wife. He demanded the money and the safe to be open, but the keys were elsewhere. Downstairs as it happens. Pammy was ordered to get out of bed and get the keys for the main safe.

Pammy was obviously shaken by all this and threw back the covers on the bed. "PUT SOME CLOTHES ON!" bellowed the masked man from the other side of the room as he caught sight of her in a Care Bears T-shirt and knickers combo. She looked at him with a hard stare. Pammy was mortified! She couldn't believe that this man actually wanted her to put more clothes on as opposed to taking them off. Also, it must be said that she had a thing about going downstairs in the club barefoot. She had never done it because of broken glass, you know? Anyway, the masked bandit has told her to get dressed and she goes down onto the floor looking for shoes. Simone, who is still at gunpoint, is trying to get the whole thing over and done with as you can imagine. "Pam, what the fuck are you doing? Just put something on your feet, please, and let's go.... he's going to kill me!"

Pammy looked up from the floor as she had one arm underneath the bed. "I know, love. I'm sorry. Just need to grab this slipper."

The gunman is getting nervous and shouts, "COME ON, LADY!" After finding the appropriate footwear to have on during an armed robbery, Pammy went downstairs and into the office to get the keys and handed over the six thousand pounds. The police swung into action but the gunmen were never seen or heard of again. They're probably living the life of Riley somewhere, hot thanks to all us pub, club and restaurant owners in Surrey!

MY OLD MAN'S A STUNTMAN

Larry Taylor, my dad, was an actor. A character actor. You'll have seen him on film and in various TV shows over the years. He's got one of those faces that makes him very recognizable. It is safe to say that looking through many of Dad's publicity photos through his career he was a very handsome man. Beautiful. Some of his early shot make him look like Errol Flynn and in later ones he morphs into Lee Marvin. He was working on a TV show called *Richard the Lionheart* at Danzinger Studios, now part of the Elstree complex, starring actor Dermot Walsh.

Ray Austin was stunt coordinator with Paddy Ryan. I went down in my school holidays to watch the filming. While I was there one of the actor/horsemen was kicked by a horse and had broken his leg very badly. Ray says to Dad, "Here, can your boy ride, Larry?" Dad never even paused for breath. "Course he can – go on, son. Get up on that horse and show Ray what you can do." So up I gets and rides around the field on this old carthorse. Without hesitation Ray gets me on board as a stunt rider on the show. Seven pounds fifty a day, another £7.50 for exploitation, in relation to the action of making use of and benefitting from a young Rocky Taylor. Then I had to ride along and get hit with a lance and fall off the horse into some peat which gave me another £7.50. Twenty-two pounds fifty a day for six weeks' work and I was fourteen years old!

Dad had worked on *Shout at the Devil* as Lee Marvin's double and had done all of the swimming for him on the picture. His success in *Zulu* in 1964 had got him back for Zulu Dawn in 1978 and this was where he met his second wife Ann. He got married and moved off to South Africa to live in Johannesburg for the rest of his life.

He was like a chameleon the way he changed his look to look like the actor he was doubling. He was in loads of TV and film right through the fifties, sixties and seventies. I got to work with him on a number of Hammer horror films at Bray Studios and on *The Persuaders*.

He was responsible for many great things in my life. I have met many great people thanks to him, but he is also responsible for one of the saddest days I will ever remember.

I'm due to take part in a celebrity golf tournament Manchester way and I'm to be partnered by my old mate, John Virgo. We're driving up in the car and John turns to me, out of the blue, and says, "How's your dad these days, Rock?" The question was very profound as I hadn't spoken to him for a couple of weeks and I thought, well, what better time than now? So, using the car phone I rang the number. The conversation went like this:

Me: "Hello, Dad."

Dad: "Rocky sweetheart, how are you?"

Me: "Yeah fine – sorry it's been so long. What you up to, then?"

Dad: "Well I've been doing…"

Long silence at the end of the phone

Me: "Dad, Dad, are you there?"

I held on for a few minutes then hung up, tried to redial but just got the busy tone. Kept trying and eventually it rang again. Then, after what seemed like an eternity, it answered.

Me: "Hello, Dad?"

Voice: "Err no it's John, I'm a neighbour of your dad's, Rocky…he's on the floor… I think he's dead!"

The very idea was just awful. Sure enough, a few minutes later the truth was confirmed. He had suffered a massive heart attack while I was in the phone to him. It doesn't matter what anyone says, nothing can prepare you for the loss of a loved one. Particularly a parent. Even if they are quite old and not in the best of health. The loss stays with you for a long time, in fact I'd say it never goes away entirely. You just learn to put it into a box in your brain, that you only go to every once in a while.

My dad was in pretty decent health. Quite active too. So, his sudden death caused much pain throughout the family.

I have many happy memories about my dad. One of which was when I was fourteen or fifteen and attending Fosdene Secondary Modern in Charlton which I believe is now a primary school. Every year they would have a talent competition, and, on this occasion, I said I would sing a song. This is obviously where my love of performing had come from. To this day I'm always happy to 'do a turn'. They asked if Dad would come along to be the judge as they knew he was in the film business.

He said he would and turned up on the day and they treated him like a big movie star. Well to me, he was. [Author's note: now that everyone has satellite TV all the old movies are being shown again. Not that long ago someone told me that three of the movies that Dad was in were on the TV at the same time. He'd have loved that.] I decided to sing a Lonnie Donegan classic *My Old Man's A Dustman*.

Some told jokes, some did a dance and others did impressions. You could cut the tension with a knife as the judge decided on the best. And guess what… I won!

WHAT'S IN A NAME?

So, as you are all aware I'm Rocky Taylor, but I was born Laurie Taylor. A good name I hear you say, why change it? Was there already a Laurie Taylor registered with Equity? Did I have to change it for financial reasons?

No! It's much simpler than that and as you'll find out a lot sillier too.

The year was 1957, Queen Elizabeth II had been on the throne for four years, skiffle music was all the rage and rock and roll was only just beginning to be played on obscure radio stations in America. The Beatles were all at school or college, and household names, like Tommy Steele, were just starting on the road to stardom.

Football was enjoying a period never before seen, with players such as Dixie Dean, Tom Finney and Stanley Matthews providing the thrills and goals to capacity crowds every week. With soccer hooligans unheard of, Saturday afternoons were regular family pilgrimages to the football club to enjoy Britain's national sport.

It was in this year that a group of young actors and performers met in 'Le Grande' coffee house in Compton Street, Soho, with the idea of starting a celebrity football team to play in Hyde Park on Sunday mornings – against all and sundry. And that is where we stayed, until some of the team started to become well known, and we moved onto a bigger stage, including Wembley and all the major stadiums in England and Europe. The team then was Jess Conrad, Sean Connery, Tommy

Steele, Harry Fowler, Andrew Ray, Antony Newley, Pete Murray and Kenny Lynch.

I was a golfer in the seventies and would play quite often. Jess Conrad and Kenny Lynch became mates and I would get asked to make the numbers up on what became the Showbiz XI football team.

We were in the dressing room one afternoon and I was surrounded by plenty of big names in showbiz. When they got announced to the crowds the place went crazy, screaming girls etc. Jess Conrad says to me, "We've got to get you a name." He thought for a few moments and then came rushing back. "I've got it, Rocky Sham the Aussie singing sensation."

I looked at him like he'd gone mad. "Rocky what? Australian? Jess, why?"

Jess, in typical Jess style, said, "Listen they don't know you from Adam, you're a stuntman you're not supposed to be recognized right? The girls will go wild when they find we've got a real-life pop star from Australia right here." Give Jess his due, he was right. Long before the days of Kylie Minogue and Jason Donovan coming over here on the back of soap opera success, I was the pop sensation from Oz who, admittedly, had never recorded a song, but was riding high on the back of made-up success.

Quite recently I saw a photograph of me in the team from 1975 with Robin Asquith, David Hamilton and Robert Lindsey. Brings back so many wonderful memories.

So, I became 'Rocky' to everyone who knew me. I eventually dropped the 'Sham' bit although Jess wanted me to keep it. It also meant that I could have my own identity. One that was separate from my dad. We often got mistaken for each other on paper. People wanted Larry and got Laurie and vice versa, but as with all actors I took on the role of Rocky Taylor and made it my own.

JESS CONRAD

We couldn't have a chapter about the Showbiz XI without a few words from the man who ran the outfit for many, many, years. Jess played for the team from 1958 until 2013. That's fifty years and in that time has raised a huge amount of money for very worthy causes. He did all this with style and grace. Oh, and not a hair out of place. Jess writes:

The one thing that gave Rocky Taylor that big break in the business was having the good fortune to look very like me. Don't get me wrong he's not as good looking as me, but then who is? His haircut was the same, he was about the same build. And back in the late fifties and early sixties I was flying high with a number of film roles. His dad, Larry, was a friend and whenever I needed a double, I'd get Rocky in. He'd fall down flights of stairs or get thrown out of windows. In fact, on one occasion in a movie called K.I.L 1 he doubled me in a fight sequence with his dad Larry. They'd worked out a routine and went through it until they were happy. Come the take and Larry punches Rocky, doubling me, then grabs both lapels and headbutts him. Problem is that on this occasion he did it for real and left Rocky cold... I mean out cold. Larry, being the true professional, took hold of Rocky and threw him through the French windows. Rocky lay there for a moment or two but came away with a terrible headache and a very apologetic father.

His ability to look like me was also a massive help when trying to fend off my legions of adoring female fans. I'd turn up at a nightclub or theatre for a show and the girls would be outside screaming my name and getting carried away by St Johns Ambulance men. To make life easier for me I got Rocky to put on my jacket and, as soon as the car stopped, he'd run out and take the flack from the girls as my car cruised round, and I got to arrive cool, calm and unruffled.

Rocky was also part of our legendary Showbiz XI football team. A team that was filled with A-list celebrities who were beating down my door to have a go. Rocky was a natural athlete. Good at every sport he tried. Football, Golf, Tennis… you name it he could do it. We had a problem at first though because he wasn't a well-known celebrity… so we made him an Australian pop star. Why? Well, back then there was no such thing as the Internet. You couldn't just Google a name and get their whole life history within seconds. Who was going to question his identity? Nobody. To be honest we could have said he was the Pope, the football going public would have lapped it up and made banners with 'We Love You Pope' on it.

He has been and remains to this day to be one of my dearest friends and still looks good today… not as good as me obviously, but pretty good.

[Author's note: The stair fall Jess is referring to was on *The Human Jungle* television series in 1964. Because I looked like Jess he got me on board as his double. So, the scene was Jess running up the stairs in this big house. At the top of the stairs was a huge mirror and the idea is Jess looks in the mirror and is scared by a demon within the mirror. With that he falls back down this long staircase. I had never done a stair fall before, didn't know how to, so I was standing at the top of the staircase and the prop master came up to me and said, "Aren't you going to use any pads for this, Rocky?"

I looked at him and asked, "Pads? What for?" I had absolutely no idea what he meant.

He said, "You can't fall down these stairs without pads. You could break your legs on this. So, come with me." He took me to the prop room and made, right in front of my eyes, knee, elbow and hip pads. From padded foam. Just enough to cushion the impact of the stairs on the way down. I did the fall and bounced down to the bottom. Once the director called "Cut!" I leaped up and felt really good. All thanks to the prop man for intervening.]

PETER BENNETT

Peter is a lovely man. A producer of the highest quality. In fact, he's been producer on *Doctor Who* for at least fifteen years if not more. We go back some time and he wanted to put in a little something for the book. Peter thank you x

'Ever since I started in the business back in 1977 Rocky was one of the favoured stuntmen, whether it was a film like James Bond or TV like Minder *he would be performing.*

'Later in my career, becoming a first assistant director and producer meant I was sometimes able to choose the stunt arranger or performer and wherever possible that would be Rocky. It's been a privilege to have known and worked with Rocky for over forty years and able to rely on him as both a top stuntman and friend.'

FAMILY

When my dad came out of the war he became an extra and would take Mum with him as they would both get a few quid. This was before anyone called it stunt work. It was action acting back then. Someone would come over and say, "Larry, you can do a punch-up, can't ya? We'll have a fight here and then roll over this and onto the floor, okay?"

Mum, Pat, was the same. Very physical. She was brought in for fights and falls to double the actresses. She also got to ride a wheelchair down a flight of stairs in the 1950 film *Room to Let* starring Jimmy Handley and Valentine Dyall as the villain. Dad had to tip Mum out of the wheelchair directly into camera. Luckily, she wasn't hurt but did get a few extra quid for having to do it three or four times. See even back then you got an adjustment. She also doubled for Honor Blackman in the 1949 film *Diamond City*.

It was a very physical household. I remember living in a prefab in Bermondsey and Dad would put me on the roof and let me roll off and he'd only catch me just before I hit the ground. Then he'd say, "Never trust anyone, son... not even your father!"

I also remember an occasion where, when we used to live in the prefabs, there were bombed buildings all around and I would go off and play with the other kids among the ruins. We'd run across the roofs, jumping from one to the other. It was literally child's play to me. The police didn't think so as the local bobby would take hold of me by the ear and march me home to tell Mum what I'd been up to. Back then as kids we didn't care. We knew about the war and the devastation that had been left, but in many kids' eyes the bombings had created new and exciting places to play.

My mum had to go out to work after Dad left and she took up numerous jobs including working on the buses as a clippie. She's ninety-three years old and to this day is still living life to the full. She likes betting on the horses, well we all do, and since I've had the opportunity and good fortune to know a few racehorse trainers in the past, this has given me an insight into the sport of kings.

Mum gets on a bus every day and goes into town to the bookies where everyone greets her. She places her bets, has a bit of lunch and catches the bus home. I've backed a few winners in my time. Sometimes I've backed them big and sometimes I've had a light flutter. These days Mum has twenty pound a day on the horses. She'll have a pound here or twenty pence there and sometimes she wins nothing, but then she might win £2,000. That's the fun of the whole thing. She loves to have something to look forward to each day and I suppose I'm the same.

Also, I should say that my mum is the best mum in the world. I know that everyone says that about their mum or dad but obviously mine IS the best. She's been so good to me over the years and I couldn't be the man I am today without her. Her love for life and her sense of fun. It all rubbed off on me. She still calls me and tells me what a good day she's having on the horses, admittedly she doesn't tell me much when she's not winning. It's always important to tell your parents that you love them. I didn't get that opportunity with my dad, but I want to make sure my mum knows that I love her. So, mum… I LOVE YOU xx

That has reminded me of one of my very first attempts at stunt work. Well, I say stunt work. That's what it would be called now, but back then I was just enjoying myself.

My uncle Bill used to work on the docks and one day, whilst I was still at school, I must have been fourteen or fifteen, he invited me down to show me what he did. He was a service engineer at Surrey Docks and would be in charge of keeping the cranes working. We stood by this huge crane and he said, "Can you see up there, at the top?" I looked up until I got an ache in my neck. I had to shield my eyes from the sun as it was a bright clear day. I told him I could see the top. He continued, "At the top of that crane is a spindle and it looks like this." In his hand was a spindle, about the size of my hand from fingertip to wrist. "Would you go up there and oil it for me?"

Well I was young and knew no fear. I took a can of grease and stuffed it into my shirt and climbed up the outside of this crane until I got to the top. I was up about fifty feet or so. I greased the spindle and then made my way back down to earth. Got to the bottom and Uncle Bill was very pleased of me. "Well done, Laurie. You did that very well indeed. You were like a monkey climbing up there. Your mum will be proud."

I always remember that and, in a strange sort of way, I've got Uncle Bill to thank for showing me that what we now call dangerous was actually child's play.

DONALD SUTHERLAND

I'd always thought Donald Sutherland was Irish and yet he was Canadian. This came as a shock to me. What didn't come as much surprise at all was his charm. I was asked to work on *Ordeal by Innocence* which was an Agatha Christie whodunit.

They asked me to drive down to Cornwall, where we would film the picture, but I had to swing round to Hammersmith and pick up Donald. He slipped into the back seat of the car, brought his hat down over his eyes and fell fast asleep. "Charming," I thought as we drove along on a wet London morning. That is exactly how everything stayed until we got to the set, around one p.m.

I woke Donald and we went on in. "I could do with some lunch, Rocky," says Donald, so I go to see what facilities are available.

"We've finished lunch, Rock," said the catering manager. "Try the Angel in the high street," he said. I wandered over to the restaurant and explained the situation. They were very happy to have us both and kept a table free. I went back and brought Donald into The Angel.

We had a good lunch: steak, potatoes, veg of all kinds and a glass or two of wine. The phone rang, and the owner came out "Rocky, you're needed back on set for rehearsals." I finished my lunch and said to Donald, "Right I'll pay half for this Donald." He looked at me over the top of his reading glasses. "Okay, Rocky, we'll sort it out."

I arrive on the set and get used to the vehicle I'll be driving, an old Wolsey. Now, the scene requires the car to lose control and bounce down the street bumping into everything on route to a wall at the very bottom.

The car was towed to the top of the road and I would steer it into this car, and bounce off that one, but I wasn't going to drive it into a wall, so I got a bunch of tyres and drove into them. With a change of camera angle, it looked like I'd hit the wall full on.

Donald appears and said, "Right then, Rocky, about this bill."

I walked over to him and said, "No problem, Donald, how much was it?" As I was saying this I was reaching for my wallet.

He looked closely at me and said, "Why don't you pay for the wine, okay?" I said this was fine as long as he was okay with it and a reassuring smile came across his face. "Good, well if you give me £450 that should cover it." My mouth fell open and hit the floor. "Four hundred and fifty quid! Seriously?"

Turns out that the two bottles were £225 each. Don't get me wrong they were good. I mean at £225 a bottle they'd have to be, right? Still Donald laughed about it for a while as he loved the panic on my face… and paid for the wine. Good bloke, Donald.

A few years later I worked with him again. I walked into the make-up trailer and there was Donald. "Donald, how are you?"

He swivels round in the chair and says, "Rocky. How are you, darling? While I think about it, I've got a bone to pick with you."

I look confused. "What about?"

He looks me straight in the eye and says, "You told everyone you made me buy the wine, when you know full well that I was always going to pay for it." I was open mouthed, "Donald, I swear to you I never told anyone that I made you pay… who makes you pay for anything? If you've been told that this happened well, I'm sorry but it's a lie."

Donald looked at me with a hard stare, then a wry smile appeared on his face. "I knew that was going to be the case, Rock. I apologize for thinking otherwise." I thanked him and turned to leave when he added, "Do you fancy a drink later?"

I stopped in my tracks, turned and said, "Can you afford it, Donald?"

I ran out of the trailer as I heard him shouting "TAYLOR!"

SEAN CONNERY

In many people's opinion Sean Connery is simply the very best actor of his generation. In mine too. He's a different breed when it comes to screen acting. I've been very lucky to work with him on several occasions. Only briefly on the Bonds, a little more on *Never Say Never Again*, but mostly on *Indiana Jones and the Last Crusade, Robin Hood Prince of Thieves* and *Highlander II*.

Indiana Jones was another great franchise that was a sure-fire hit. Steven Spielberg and George Lucas had taken the idea of Bond and re-worked it for a whole new audience. I'd worked on *Raiders of the Lost Ark* as an actor and stuntman. I had doubled Harrison Ford in a number of the riding scenes before he jumps onto and under the truck holding the 'Ark'. That wasn't me it was Terry Leonard. I was one of the mine guards getting disposed of by Indy in *Temple of Doom*, but I was Sean Connery's double during the bike chase, tank chase and fireplace blaze on *Last Crusade*.

There's a very famous photo of me and Sean stood next to each other for continuity on the set. He is a bit taller than me, and we are hardly identical, but when we are wearing the same clothes and once the action starts on the film set it is difficult to spot the difference. This is the key to the stunt performer, as looking like the person you are doubling is a bonus. When the camera rolls I must become Sean, I must take on his persona and therefore become a good double.

June 1st 1988 and I'm on set to perform a major fire sequence. In the movie Indy and his dad, Connery, are back to back on two chairs, tied together with ropes. Sean takes Indy's lighter from his pocket, trying to burn through the ropes. Burns himself, drops the lighter and sets fire to the carpet, curtains, in fact the whole room before long is ablaze. They bounce into the fireplace for protection. That's how the scene read on the page. We now had to create this for real on the set.

Vic Armstrong was the film's stunt coordinator and was Harrison Ford's double, but on this occasion, Harrison would be doing the sequence himself. The set was rigged in such a way that we knew exactly what was to light up first. Harrison and I bounced our way across the room and into the fireplace. When the sequence was finished all the members of the crew stood up and applauded. Spielberg, Lucas and Connery all stood and applauded. It was very emotional. Why? Well someone had told them that this was a very significant day.

I had my accident on *Death Wish III* at four p.m. on 19 June 1985 and here I was 19 June 1988 at four p.m. doing my first fire job since that day.

Sean had been very good to me and we'd got to know each other on set. We both had a level playing field with our love of golf and we'd talk for hours about the game, our swing and old golfing stories. Once we'd finished this picture Sean was going off to do a cameo appearance in Kevin Costner's Robin Hood movie, *Prince of Thieves*. Now, when I say cameo I mean four minutes' screen time, but his inclusion in the film, playing King Richard, would assist with the global distribution of the film. I was once again brought in as his double. An odd credit as he was seen getting off a horse, but a great deal of footage was cut showing me riding the horse across the countryside before Sean arrives for his close-up. On the strength of this I was off to do *Highlander II* in Argentina and Sean had asked for me to go along as his double.

I was loving this period in my life, being Sean's double. Not a bad addition to any CV. I'm getting myself ready and was in the process of packing when the phone rang. I answered it and found myself talking to a production assistant who said there had been a change of plan and another stuntman was going in my place to double Sean! This was awful for me as I'd got myself all ready and then to have this at the eleventh hour was a real body blow.

So, I decided to ring Sean and ask if he knew anything about it. I'd known him long enough to be in a position to call him at his home in Spain from time to time. The phone rang "Yessshh?" It was Sean.

"Sean, it's Rocky." I waited to hear his response, to make sure I'd got his full attention.

"Rocky, how are you? What can I do for you?" I explained that I was all ready to go to Argentina and that I had received a call from the production company saying I wasn't needed. "What!" The response was just what I'd hoped for. "Don't worry about anything," he said. "I'll sort this out."

I hung up and was much happier. A few days later the phone rang, and it was another production assistant from the film company. "Mr Taylor, I'm calling about *Highlander II*. Mr Connery has asked for you by name to accompany him on this production as his double. If you are ready, we'll send a car for you on Wednesday and take you to the airport." This was Sean at his very best. I was collected and travelled first class to Argentina. Not only was I Sean's double but was also the sword master in charge of sword fights on the picture.

I met Sean a few days later and he was charming and professional as ever. "Did you bring your clubs with you?"

It was a time in my life where I took my clubs everywhere with me. I liked golf very much and had been playing quite a bit. I thought, what an honour. Playing golf with Sean Connery! "Yes, Sean, I have – where are we going to play?"

He chuckled to himself and said, "Well in fact I've been asked to play a pro-celebrity round with Lee Travino on Saturday and I wanted to know if I could use yours?"

Well seeing as it was Sean I couldn't refuse him. He returned a few days later after coming third in this celebrity golf tournament. "The only reason I played so well was because of your clubs, you know," Sean said when he returned them. A gent through and through. In hindsight I should have told him I'd caddy for him. I'd have happily walked around after him. He's got that sort of energy about him, wherever you are people just want to be near him.

Jimmy Tarbuck played golf with Sean quite often and told a lovely story about what 'Big Tam' is like on the course. [Author's note: Sean Connery was born Thomas Sean Connery and was known as 'Big Tam' by his friends and family.] He was playing one day and wasn't playing very well. We've all been there, but anyway he decided that after another terrible fairway shot he was done for the day. So, he took his five iron and bent it over his knee. Did the same thing in the other direction and threw both pieces into the undergrowth. If you've ever tried to do this, it's almost impossible. On another occasion he was playing and both players had lost their balls in the rough. "You go and search for the ball," says Sean.

A moment later Tarby finds a ball. "I found mine, Sean. It's a Titleist 1."

Sean shouts over, "That's my ball. Is there anything else on it?"

Jimmy says, "No there's nothing else on it. It's my ball."

Sean was still not satisfied. "Just look again you may have missed something." Jimmy was just about to throw the ball back onto the fairway when he turned the ball around. On the back was embossed on the ball '007'.

PIERCE BROSNAN

If there was ever a man who was born to play Bond, it was Pierce. I met him briefly on the Bond film *For Your Eyes Only* when he visited the set with his wife Cassandra Harris who was playing a role in the picture. He was easy going, good looking and a fair footballer too. He was a favourite with the Broccolis who were waiting for him to finish his contract with *Remington Steele*.

Pierce joined the team as 007 in 1995 on *Goldeneye*. I was doing a television series called *The Governor* at the time but saw the movie and loved it. Thought he was great and very well cast. So, for his second outing as Bond *Tomorrow Never Dies* I was called in by Vic Armstrong to take a role in the film as a 'heavy'. Me, Terry Richards, Romo Gorrara, Neil Finnaghan and Terry Plummer would be involved in a good old-fashioned dust-up during a live TV broadcast.

Pierce was very handy during a fight, sold his punches and reacted well to ours. We're giving him a right good kicking, when he ducks out of the way of a punch that gets Neil and from then on, the fight is in his favour. This fight takes place in a music studio which is soundproofed. So as Terry Plummer sits watching the broadcast of the villain Elliott Carver on TV in the control booth sipping his coffee, all hell is breaking loose behind him in the studio. I'm being hit with a cello, Neil is getting hit with a lamp. We did a thing where Bond and I had to crash through the control booth window where Terry was sitting. Wayne Michaels doubled Pierce and we ran headlong at this window, smashing it into a million pieces and landing at Terry's feet.

To add insult to injury I then get on the radio and try and alert the villain's henchman, but just as I'm getting through Bond comes up and smashes a big ashtray over my head. "Rocky are you sure about this?" asks a worried Pierce during our rehearsal,

"Look don't worry, they made it big enough to get a good grip on it without any chance of you cracking over the head with your fist." I tried to reassure him… he didn't seem that convinced to be honest, but when it came to the take, he strolled up, bold as you like, played about with the ashtray as he approached me, then CRASH! Right on the mark. I slump to the floor, job done.

He comes up afterwards. "I didn't get you, did I?" It was so convincing that he thought he punched me on the head as he brought his fist down.

"Pierce, it's fine, really you did great."

He looked at me and says, "But you went down very quickly, I thought I'd got you for real."

I smiled and said, "I was acting, Pierce."

Can I also say that I thought my German accent was world class on that movie? "Heir Stamper vee cannot get into zee car." Is that German? Well I was convinced and so was Roger Spottiswoode. Which is all that matters, right? [Author's note: Roger Spottiswoode was the director of the eighteenth James Bond adventure *Tomorrow Never Dies.]*

We also got to work together on the driving sequences around the multistory car park. We filmed this sequence at the Brent Cross shopping centre in London and had great fun. I was passenger in a Mercedes chasing Bond's BMW 750, full of gadgets and gizmos. The final part of the sequence has our Mercedes on a ratchet. I should point out what that is really. The wire is attached to the car and will stop the car dead in its tracks, causing the occupants to be thrown forward.

The BMW crashes from the roof and lands in a hire car shop window and the Mercedes crashes through the wall of the multistory and is left dangling.

Also, on that film I got to work with my great mate Romo Gorrara. Sadly, this was his last film. He was diagnosed with cancer a while before and was still undergoing treatment when he'd been asked to work on the picture, but fair play to him he was as professional as ever and a lovely fella. He died a few weeks later. Pierce wanted in on the action one day as we were getting our photos taken for continuity. He jumped in the middle of us and the result is a photo I will always cherish.

BROOKE SHIELDS

In 1982 I got chance to work on a film called *Sahara* starring Brooke Shields. I played Kamal and Greg Powell played Abdullah. We spent eight weeks in Israel and we were given the job by her mum Teri, of looking after Brooke. If she wanted to go out we'd go with her and just make sure she came to no harm, after all she was one of the most beautiful women in the world and attracted a fair amount of attention from any male who happened to walk by. She was really lovely, a good kid and always full of fun. She was eighteen, impossibly beautiful and I was responsible for her!

Subsequently we got on very well and she would ask for me if she was to attend events. Teri would include me as 'the minder' and I kept a look out for her. One such occasion was in London and Brooke was due to appear at that year's Royal Variety Performance to sing on stage with Bob Hope. I arrived at her hotel, went up in the lift and knocked at the door of the suite. Teri answered and told me Brooke was just getting ready. I sat down and chatted with Teri for a few moments then, in through the door, came Brooke.

Have you ever had one of those moments where your brain and your mouth just don't keep up with each other? I have. My head was filled with this vision standing before me. The way the room was lit caused her to be surrounded by a bright haze. She looked absolutely beautiful. "Rocky... are you okay?" she said as she stood regally in front of me.

"Oh yes... you look stunning... beautiful... wow," I added.

I then realized her lips were moving but I couldn't hear the words. I shook my head and heard her say, "So you can be my date for the night, okay?"

So, there I was. I was Brooke Shield's date for the evening. I was to escort her to the London Palladium. As jobs go this is one of the very best. We took the lift down to the lobby and I have never seen so many photographers in my life. Flash bulbs popped, paparazzi shouted, "Brooke, this way!" Then it dawned on me that they were taking photos of us! Unbelievable!

So, we get to the Palladium and more press are waiting for us outside. We get in, down a corridor to an L-shaped room where Bob Hope is waiting for her. So, I turn her round to face me and say, "Okay, darling, in you go, you'll be brilliant."

A wry smile appeared on her face. "You come in with me, Rocky. I'd be happier if you came in too." So, I go in with her.

Bob embraces her and gives her a kiss. "You look beautiful," he says. "Now it's all gonna be just great. I arrive on stage in a car, you arrive on stage in a car and we'll sing the song just as we rehearsed it, okay?" She nodded, and he looked at me and nodded. "And you are...?" He held out a hand to me.

"Oh, I'm a stuntman, sir, but I'm here to escort my friend Brooke."

Hope threw his hands up in the air. "Isn't that great? Glad you could make it... I'll take care of her for ya, okay?"

We left Bob and walked back down the corridor to another room where some of the press had gathered for questions and photos. The PR guy had asked Brooke if it was okay to have some questions. She turns to him and said, "Go through, Rocky." So now I'm mediating on behalf of the world's press and the most beautiful woman in the world!

The PR guy announces to the press, "Direct all of your questions through Mr Taylor please. Right first question."

This guy at the back says, "Rocky, is it okay to ask Brooke about her time here in London and what else she plans to do while she's here?"

I turn to Brooke, "You okay with that?"

She looks at me "Okay."

I point at the man who asked the question. "Yes, that's fine."

"Great," he said before asking the same question at Brooke! This went on for an hour!

She was falling about laughing and knew exactly how to have fun with someone.

Anyway, all worked out well and I went into the theatre and sat with Teri on the front row. She handed me a bottle of tonic water. I took a good slug. Then discovered that it's actually vodka and tonic and it's about three parts vodka, to one-part tonic! Which took the edge off, I can tell you.

We've remained firm friends for the last thirty years. She is not only an incredibly beautiful woman and a very fine actress, but a really nice person. That is very important in this day and age.

Quite a few years later Greg (Powell) and me, were invited to Brooke's birthday party in London at Green Mint. Our wives came and the only person we knew in the room was Brooke Shields. We were ushered into this private room out the back and ate a spectacular Indian meal.

Then someone stood up and started giving a speech telling us how wonderful she is, then they sat down and someone else got up and started telling a story about Brooke. Now Greg is saying to me, "When you getting up, Rock? Go on, you tell a story." I kept waving him away as I didn't really have anything to say in particular and I didn't want to say anything out of turn.

Anyway, a few more speeches go by and, just as everyone thinks the speeches are all over, I jump up from my seat. My wife Pammy and Greg's wife Dawn looked at me, looked at each other and sank down into their seats, then put their heads in their hands! But when I stood up, I realized I'd got nothing new to say that the rest hadn't already said. But I was up now and the whole room was looking at me. I had to do something. I did the only thing I could have done under the circumstances. I sang *Delilah*. It's got me out of one or two scrapes in the past, why not now? As I was part way through verse one, I also noticed that everyone in the room was looking at one another all trying to find out who the drunken idiot was who was stood up singing an old Tom Jones hit. Pammy and Dawn were now under the table, refusing to come out. Greg was in tears laughing and the only other person in the room who was howling with laughter was Brooke Shields… thank God for that.

HANDS ACROSS THE SEA BY BROOKE SHIELDS

The filming of the movie *Sahara* took me and my mother and my dog Jack all over Israel and Puerto Rico. It was an 'adventure' film which meant that there were going to be many action scenes and lots of stunts. I always loved doing stunts and stuntmen in general follow a strong code of safety, look after one another, protect those they are doubling, and love the danger of it all. They are a breed unto themselves and "Men Men" as my mother would say.

It was day one of filming and Rocky and Greg came up to me on set and introduced themselves. They would be playing two Bedouin 'bad guys' who kidnap me in the desert and there would be horses, guns and stunts, oh my! They were quite gentlemanly and explained that they were not only my stunt team but basically the ones I should go to should anybody bother me. Their accents just added to the excitement of it all. This was going to be fun! At lunch that day I sat with them and instantly Rocky and I began making each other laugh. I knew I had found a friend.

As a kid on movie sets, one needs guardians and as a first line of defence. Very quickly my mom singled out Rocky and Greg to be my front lines. She asked them to keep an eye on me, not just on set, but after wrap each day as well. Mainly, this entailed us dancing to *Come on Eileen* in the hotels and nightclub-hopping like little kids without a care in the world. We became regulars and our favourite songs would immediately start playing when we entered the room.

For this film, the stunts were hard, but I threw myself into any of the ones the boys would let me do. They taught me how to shoot guns, hop on and off horses, kick bad guys, punch other bad guys, and drive vintage cars in the sand. We had a blast and even when we all got caught in a horrible sandstorm that left our mouths, ears, eyes, hair, coated with sand, we managed to laugh.

One day one of the other actors who was less inclined towards any kind of physical activity, decided to try doing his own stunt. He was supposed to leap onto my horse and ride with me off into the sunset. On his first try, he jumped onto my horse and used me for leverage, pulling me down and clean off the horse, landing smack on my back onto an apple box that had been placed there to help him jump higher. Rocky was watching the whole thing and when I hit the ground doubled over in pain, Rocky's face became instantly crimson with rage. I could swear I saw steam coming out of his ears. He ran to me with an ice pack that seemed to materialize out of thin air, scolded the actor, and got me to my feet. Then, even through my tears, Rocky managed to put a smile on my face.

That's just who he is.

The conclusion of filming brought about tears and hugs and promises to keep in touch. And we have done just that for over thirty years.

During that time, I had a collection of hands made from ivory, marble, wood, anything I could find. As a wrap gift Rocky gave me a beautiful big silver charm of a handshake and we coined our friendship "Hands Across the Sea," which I wear to this day.

Then one year I was going to Bob Hope's eightieth birthday in London and my mom asked Rocky if he would escort me from the Mayfair Hotel to the London Palladium. The paparazzi were insane, and I could tell that Rocky was a bit shocked and on high alert. That evening, I actually got to teach him something. I put a big smile on my face and, through my teeth, told him how to navigate the insanity as quickly as possible and without incident. It felt good to share knowledge with him for a change.

We then went on to do another film together and had just as much fun.

Years later, while performing *Chicago* in the West End, I celebrated my fortieth birthday. Greg and Rocky came to my dinner party with their amazing other halves. My husband flew in from NYC and surprised me. Chris had not met 'my boys' but had heard all the stories. Now here they were, all in the same room, laughing and drinking red wine and my heart jumped for joy. My baby Rowan was two and she was adoring the attention she was getting and, as I held her and looked at the array of people from all over the world, and varying walks of life who had assembled to meet one another and raise a toast to our friendship, I was reminded of just how blessed I was... and continue to be. Time nor distance can soften true bonds of friendship. Thanks Rock!

STANLEY BAKER

Stanley was one of my dad's best friends. They did a lot together. Worked on films, socialized and generally remained good pals. I got to work with him on a production for the BBC in 1974. *Robinson Crusoe* was to be one of his last projects. I would be his double, tea boy and general dog's body, but I didn't mind that. We'd nearly finished filming and he says, "Rocky, I'm going to do *Zulu Dawn*, you interested in working on it with me?" Interested? My dad was in *Zulu* with Stanley and to work on a new project with him would have been great. I told him I was available, and he gave me the thumbs up.

Stanley was always into something. He was a bit of a rogue and… well a villain at heart. He liked a freebie and wasn't afraid of bending the rules to get it. Well he'd struck some deal with BMW who'd given him two or three free cars. He rang me and said, "You drive don't you… I've got a great job for you, make you a few quid." He wanted me to drive from Scotland down the country stopping at all the BMW showrooms along the way and seeing how good the sales staff were at their jobs. A bit like a secret shopper.

I visited every showroom nationwide and got £500 quid here and a grand or so there, turned out to be a very nice way to make a few quid. Stanley was thrilled and when I got back from my trip in 1975, he said, "Well done, Rocky. Don't forget *Zulu Dawn*."

I said, "Stanley, how could I? I won't forget, I'm looking forward to it."

Three months later he was dead. Cancer had kicked in and he died in his villa in Spain.

ROBERT WAGNER

Hart to Hart was a very successful TV show here in the UK and during the height of success the production came to London to film. My friend Alan Stuart was the stunt coordinator and I was to double Robert Wagner in a few scenes, one of which called for a fight on a pontoon next to Lambeth Bridge. We'd rehearsed the sequence over a period of time and the final payoff was to see me, doubling Wagner, fall over the side of the pontoon into the Thames and apparently drown. One morning I turned up on the set and was told that Mr Wagner, who was also the producer, would like to see me in his caravan. I walked up and knocked on the door. "You wanted to see me sir," I said.

Mr Wagner took a moment then leaned forward on the couch. "You're doing the stunt doubling me today, right?" I nodded. "How much are you getting paid for this stunt?"

I did a quick mental calculation in my head. "Err, £500 was the agreed fee, sir, for the fight and then the fall into the water."

He made notes then looked at me again. "Okay, your £500 is safe, that's yours, but just the fight okay? I don't want the drowning sequence in."

I agreed and that's what happened. A fall into the water was filmed later on, but a planned sequence of me doubling him in a drowning sequence was never used.

Later on, he signed an autograph to me which said, *Rocky you are the best and you sure made me look good – well not that good – Bollocks!*

Lovely man.

RICHARD BURTON

In 1971 I worked on a gangster movie called Villain with Richard Burton. One sequence I was doubling for an actor called John Hallam who was a getaway driver after Burton's gang rob a security van. So, the sequence has us attacking the guards, smashing the van, piling into the car and away. I'm driving, Richard Burton is next to me and another actor called Del Henney was sat next to him, plus we had three in the back.

So, on action I go for it following the camera car, police shoot and the tyre is hit. I swerve to the left hitting parked cars, I swerve to the right hitting more parked cars and, in my ear, Mr Burton is screaming, "Fucking hell! What you trying to do fucking kill me? Fuck sake!"

I slide the car to a stop and everyone looks at me. The director comes back to us and looks in through the window. "Rocky, what's the matter? Why did you stop?" I told him that Mr Burton was screaming, and he thought that I was going to kill him... stunned silence... followed by laughter.

The director said, "Take a look down there." He pointed to the floor of the car by the dashboard. Sure enough there was a microphone. "You stupid bastard... he's acting!"

I got a chance to work with him again years later on *The Wild Geese* in South Africa. He was the leader of the mercenary unit sent to snatch back the jailed president, Limbani, from the clutches of the current dictator.

We'd been out there a little while getting used to the heat and training. Each night, at eight p.m., we'd make our way to the dining room for a meal with the cast and other members of the crew. Roger Moore and his wife came in, then Richard Harris, Hardy Kruger and finally Richard Burton. As he walked in, he shouts, "Where's Rocky? Where's Rocky Taylor?" The room fell silent as someone directed him my way "Ah, Rocky, I knew your father you know. Yes, good man – he's coming out to the house when we get back for the weekend you must come too." He walked off in the direction of the bar… the room was now not only silent, but all were looking at me. That was the power of the man. Able to silence the room in the blink of an eye. He was a class act. Random fact for you: whilst we were out on location, we were joined by none other than actor, choreographer, tap dancer and television presenter Lionel Blair. Yeah. I know! Turns out he was mates with my dad. In the same party that turned up was Jimmy Edwards a fine old comedian and actor. All pals with my dad.

Incidentally, on that picture Bob Simmons had brought us out to take on the action sequences. A big one was on a bridge over a dry riverbed where our convoy of trucks and men is attacked by a plane that drops a bomb which blows up and engulfs one of the trucks in flames. Greg Powell and George Cooper were on the bridge and were set alight. Usually in a situation like this, once the stunt is complete the safety crew would go in and douse the stuntmen using fire extinguishers. But here was a bit different.

Out of shot was a large inflatable pool. A bit like a paddling pool only a bit bigger. When the director shouted "Cut!" George and Greg would, no pun intended but, hotfoot it out of shot and fall into the pool putting out the flames. Facilities were so primitive in that region of South Africa at the time that everything was very Heath Robinson.

STUNT CHALLENGES

In 1982 I was asked to take part in a show for ITV where stuntmen would compete against one another over a series of challenges to see who the best was. My old mate Lewis Collins was presenting the show, and all this would be filmed down on the back lot at Pinewood Studios.

Martin Grace, Richard Graydon, Mike Potter, Eddie Eddon, Willie Morgan, Nick Gillard and I all took part and had to jump a motorcycle over an obstacle then slide it under a limbo pole, jump thirty feet from a roof, jousting and a car challenge. The stuntman with the most points was the winner and, what do you know? I only go and win the bloody thing! Well, Lewis presented me with a lovely cup and it was well received on the TV when it was shown later on in the year.

The success of this first show led the makers of *Stunt Challenge* to crack on with a second show the following year. I was asked to perform a one of a kind gag. I had to drive a car under a trailer where the roof would come off, then I'd drive the roofless car up a ramp and roll it over. This was going to take some doing, but what a stunt!

We'd prepped the car so when it hit the trailer the roof would come off easily, providing I had plenty of momentum. The tricky part was rolling the car over without a roof. A car turnover relies on there being a roof to roll onto or over on. The stuntman also relies on the roll cage that is placed inside the car and around the roof which will prevent the roof from caving in upon impact. So, when you don't have a roof or a roll cage, it becomes very dangerous indeed.

I opted to have handholds to push against as the car rolled over. These kept me against the seats and would prevent me from falling onto the ground and being crushed by the car I was driving. The car went up the ramp and began to roll. I saw sky followed by ground followed by pitch black. The next thing I remember is the other stunt guys and the safety boys rolling the car over before Derek Thompson, who was presenting, stuffed a mic in my face and asked how I felt after my stunt. I was beaten into second place this year behind Roy Alon, who reversed a van through an articulated lorry.

Well, I was on a roll so with that in mind I went on to do the following year's show as well. The stunts were getting bigger and better with each year. I was to drive my car in and out of many other vehicles, roll it over, then get set on fire. It went well and looked great on screen, but I was beaten again by Greg Powell who was rolling an articulated lorry.

I was to have taken part in 1985 but my injury on *Death Wish III* prevented me from taking place. I was to pipe roll a car through the side of a lorry which would have been one hell of a ride, I can tell you. Greg Powell took my place and did it for me and did a great job, too.

They were good days and I believe they got the format right after the first year. It became more of a storyboard action sequence than a contest to find who the best was. Sadly, it all came to an end after the accident on *The Late Late Breakfast Show* where a member of the public was killed. From that moment on, *Stunt Challenge* was no more.

Rocky Taylor in costume as Sean Connery's stunt double on the 1991 film *Highlander 2: The Quickening*, standing beside the film's star Christopher Lambert.

Rocky Taylor in costume as Sean Connery's stunt double on the 1991 film *Highlander 2: The Quickening*.

Rocky Taylor on the set of the 1982 film *Sahara*, starring Brooke Shields.

ROCKY TAYLOR (STUNT MAN)

Rocky Taylor seen jumping from a burning
building in the 1985 film *Death Wish 3*.

Rocky Taylor being carried away from the heat of the burning building after his fall on *Death Wish 3* by stuntmen Jazzer Jeyes and Tom Delmar.

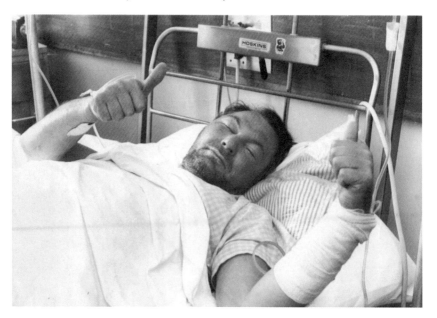

Rocky in 1985 lying in his hospital bed after the accident on *Death Wish 3*.

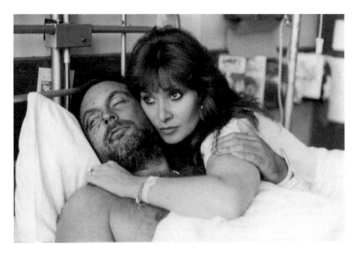

Rocky in his hospital bed being looked
after by his then partner, Marlene.

Rocky Taylor previously unseen publicity stills from the early 1970s.

Rocky standing with his great friend and fellow stuntman, Dinny Powell.

On the set of the 1981 film *Raiders of the Lost Ark*. L-R stuntmen Paul Weston, Terry Leonard, Glenn Randall, Billy Horrigan, Rocky Taylor, Peter Diamond and Sergio Mioni.

Rocky playing a guard being attacked and killed twice by Sean Connery as James
Bond in the 1983 film, *Never Say Never Again*

JESS CONRAD

Is our goalkeeper. He became famous after appearing in a T.V. play called "ROCK-A-BYE BARNEY". Stage, T.V. and film appearances followed. Jess topped the Poll in I.T.V.'s "WHAM!!" His latest movies include "TOO YOUNG TO LOVE" and "KONGA". Latest T.V. play "SOMEONE WHO CARES" (B.B.C.). Jess has a recording contract with "Decca". Jess is also now appearing in the new I.T.V. series called "The Odd Man".

LARRY TAYLOR

Actor—what else can he say! Has not made a record yet. Has featured in more than 30 major films—westerns and anywhere where big uglies are needed—T.V., stage and screen. Just completed "SWISS FAMILY ROBINSON", in "TRINIDAD", "THE SINGER NOT THE SONG", "SPAIN". Help—is at present resting.

BERNARD BRESSLAW

Bernard, an actor of long standing, became a big name overnight through "The Army Game". He made his record debut on HMV with "MAD PASSIONATE LOVE" and since then has made three films, the latest being "THE UGLY DUCKLING". Centre-half or reserve goal-keeper, Bernard used to play rugby before turning to football and is a master of the drop kick. Two pantomimes and play "MASTER OF NONE". On tour in variety. In September started new series for B.B.C. T.V.

MALCOLM ALLISON

Former skipper West Ham United, was forced to give up professional soccer after a major operation. Was asked to join T.V. All Stars last season for whom he enjoys playing as much as his pro days. This season he is player-coach.

A programme from a Celebrity XI match, featuring many of the biggest names in entertainment at the time, including one Larry

A signed photo of Rocky Taylor and Brooke Shields on the set of *Sahara* [1982].

Rocky Taylor's father, Larry Taylor, in publicity stills from the mid-1960s.

Rocky Taylor doubling for Patrick MacNee as John Steed on the television series, *The Avengers*.

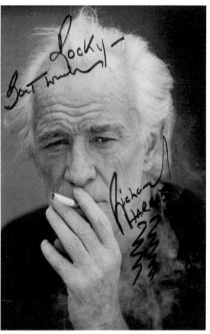

Rocky with the actor Michael Elphick, on the set of the Central Television drama, *Boon*, in 1989.

Signed photographer dedicated to Rocky from the late actor Richard Harris.

Rocky slumped at the feet of actress Carmen Du Sautoy after a very tiring fight on the set of the 1974 James Bond adventure, *The Man with The Golden Gun*.

Rocky Taylor and fellow stunt performer, Elaine Ford, attend a cast and crew screening of *Indiana Jones and the Last Crusade* with the film's star, Harrison Ford.

On the set of the 1981 film, *Raiders of the Lost Ark*. Rocky Taylor in the driving position next to his friend and fellow stuntman, Romo Gorrara.

On the set of the 1989 film *Indiana Jones and the Last Crusade* Rocky Taylor doubling for Sean Connery standing with the film's director Steven Spielberg.

Rocky Taylor playing an Arab heavy about to kill Sir John Mills on the set of the 1982 film, *Sahara*.

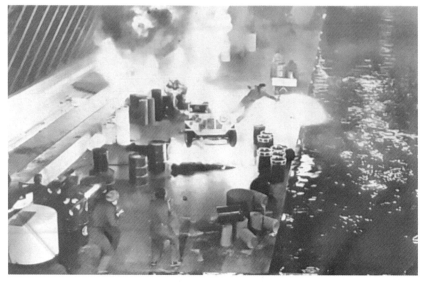

On the 007 stage set for the 1977 James Bond adventure, *The Spy Who Loved Me*. Rocky driving the yellow Mini Moke. Beside him is stuntman Jimmy Lodge and leaping from the car is stuntman Paul Weston.

Larry Taylor and Nosher Powell, both sadly no longer with us.

On the set of the 2002 James Bond adventure *Die Another Day* with the star of the film Pierce Brosnan.

JOHN LANDIS

I'd worked with John on two occasions. Firstly, on *American Werewolf in London* during the chaos in Piccadilly Circus at the end of the picture, then years later on a film called *Spies Like Us* starring Chevy Chase and Dan Ackroyd. My initial memory is of me doubling Dan Ackroyd and Peter Brace doubling Chevy Chase being taken on the back of a skidoo to a remote point a mile from anywhere. The purpose of this was that we could get one of the classic shots in the film: two lonely figures walking in a world of snow.

Every time we took one step forward we went down a further foot and a half! It was one of the most exhausting shoots I've ever been on.

During that shoot, horses would be used. During a gun battle, horses would rear up and generally act up whilst I, who was one of the assembled soldiers, was ducking for cover. It struck me that the more the scene went on, the more frantic the horses became which on icy roads meant a real possibility of injury. "Cut!" shouted Landis. "Again!" he boomed, and everyone went back to the number one position.

I'd seen enough of these and just before we started, I shouted, "Okay that's enough – someone is going to get injured or killed if we carry on like this!"

What seemed like an eternity went by before another voice said, "Okay, that's it for the day, folks, thank you."

I was in my hotel room that night and there was a knock on the door. I opened it and there was John Landis. "Were you the one who spoke up during today's shoot?"

I nodded. "Yes, sir, I was, it was getting way too dangerous out there."

He looked at me, cleared his throat and said, "Let me tell you something, pal, nobody uses that word on my set, nobody."

I looked bemused. "What word?" I waited for his response.

"You said that someone was going to get killed if this carried on – you know I'm being sued by the families on *The Twilight Zone* for millions of dollars. You know what a statement like that could do to me?"

I looked over his shoulder at Paul Weston, the stunt coordinator, who had his head in his hands. "Mr Landis sir, I apologize. That wasn't my intention at all. I just wanted to make sure everyone was safe during the sequence. After all, safety is so important now."

I paused expecting to be sacked off the picture and shown the door, but he looked at me and said, "Okay, but just think about what you're saying first, eh?"

I nodded. "Yes, sir, I will and thanks."

Paul Weston stood in the doorway as everyone had gone and shook his head – he knew I was inches away from the flight home. "See you tomorrow, Rocky," he said, which was quite reassuring.

TITANIC

I was at home one day when the phone rang. It was Simon Crane's assistant asking if I could go up to town for an audition for *Titanic*. I was to audition for the role of a stoker in the engine room which fellow stuntman Derek Lea got in the end. So anyway, I did that, went home and thought nothing of it until the phone rang a day or two later. I was told I hadn't got the role I'd auditioned for, but Mr Cameron wanted me to play the part of Bert Cartmel. He is the passenger with his wife and daughter who are all killed in the sinking.

I thought it was brilliant to get a job like this, so they gave me a date to go and, in the meantime, I went off to La Manga in Spain to play a charity golf match. Whilst out there I got a call to say production had been brought forward and I had to be on the next plane to Mexico to start shooting. I even left my wife Pamela there, so I could fly home, pack and set off for Mexico.

I flew out first class, which was lovely, thanks to Virgin Airlines. I got to San Diego and then was taken down into Mexico and onto the set at Fox's Baja studio. The first thing I saw was the ship. A façade, but nevertheless simply astounding to see something that big in front of you. My mouth dropped open at the site of the *Titanic* right there.

Every day when I arrived on set I had to pinch myself to make sure it wasn't all a dream. To get an opportunity to work on this ship every night was a dream come true. What a job the production team had done too. The ship was resting in a tank, which was thirty feet deep and along its hull was a gimbal which is a hydraulic system allowing them to tilt the position of the ship for the sinking sequence.

I found Simon Crane, the stunt coordinator, who told me I would be on the picture for six months, which was great news. We did quite well out of that as we were being paid on a weekly basis into an account and, the day before we were due to leave, we all decided to take the money home in cash. I was also, as you can imagine, a little worried about bringing it through the border as on the way down they took my brand-new set of golf clubs off me. I thought if they can take a set of clubs off me, what will they do with hard-earned cash!? Well I can tell you that my arse was hanging out the entire time in customs and, to this day, I have no idea how they missed it.

Anyway, where was I? Oh yes, the ship… the camera is on the docks with the ship and thousands of people waving it off. The camera pans across the crowd and up to the cargo deck where a car is being hoisted on board. The camera continues to pan before finally coming to rest on my face. I have my daughter in my arms and my wife by my side. "Do you like that boat, darling," I say to the little one.

"That's not a boat, Daddy, it's a ship," she says and there you have little old me speaking the first lines in one of the biggest films of all time. Then, at the end during the dream sequence where Rose is remembering all the people she met on the ship, I'm on the stairs with my daughter in my arms.

I'm in the picture five times altogether, but I leave you to find me. It was a truly wonderful experience to work on. Six twelve-hour shifts a week, six p.m. till six a.m. Great crew, fine cast and memories that will last with me forever.

I will say that this was also a very dark period for me as I've never been on a production that was so real. The drowning sequences where we all had to go into and under the water were challenging, yes, but more than that they were mentally very moving.

I would regularly get flashbacks and images in my mind of those poor people who died when the *Titanic* sank for real all those years ago. I remember waking up in a cold sweat some nights after having nightmares about drowning for real in the water. This was the brilliance

97

of the production, I guess. The fact that they could create something so real that even the crew could get those cold shivers and that eerie sense of unease every time we filmed those sinking sequences. Well I did anyway. I don't think I'll ever work on a picture with that magnitude again.

[Author's note: In remembering my time on this movie I remember that we used to get a minibus from the hotel to the set every day. Well it was nice that the production company had laid this on, but it was a bit cramped and not very comfortable. So, one day I decided I would buy a car, which I did. A beautiful red Pontiac convertible. I drove fellow stuntmen Paul Heasman and Lee Sheward to and from the set. And when we had finished the movie I just sold the car to a guy in the street. He was looking for a good runner. This car was a great runner, very cool and made all the worries of the world disappear when you shifted gear. He bought it for $50. A steal.]

SIR BEN KINGSLEY

Now then I have worked with Sir Ben Kingsley on two occasions. Firstly, on *Sexy Beast* as the stunt coordinator which was not only great fun to do, but very satisfying too. It really means a lot when you see the finished film and know that you've done the very best you could have done. Then I worked with him on a picture called *BloodRayne* in Romania.

Incidentally he has to be called 'Sir Ben'… no seriously he does. On the call sheet it had 'Sir Ben'. So, when you saw him in the morning it was always "Good morning, Sir Ben," which I didn't have a problem with as I call everyone sir, primarily because I can't remember their names!

We were all issued with phones for our time on set and I was sitting in the hotel one day when the phone went. "Hello Rocky… it's Sir Ben here." I didn't need to know who it was as I would recognize his voice anywhere, but he went on, "I'm sure you understand the phrase 'movie magic' and how we create something wonderful out of something not so wonderful." I'll be honest I was a bit bemused by what he was trying to tell me, but I let him run with it. "You know when you have a sword fight and both actors are doubled?" I nodded as it was the first time during the conversation that I knew what he was talking about. "Well that nutter Michael Madsen broke my finger last time we had a sword fight together and I do not want to see him brandishing a sword in this film."

This was a tricky request as they both had a fairly lengthy sword fight to undertake towards the end of the picture. But ever the trooper I found a good double for 'Sir Ben' and a good double for Mr Madsen. So, in the finished film whenever you can see either 'Sir Ben' or Michael the opponent is always a double. Therefore, keeping everyone happy and getting the end result.

PETER O'TOOLE

Another one of my heroes and in 1988 I got to work with him on a Neil Jordan picture called *High Spirits*. I suppose he'd always been one of 'the lads': him, Richard Harris and Oliver Reed. When I worked with him he was nothing but a gentleman, smoked like a train, but with style and grace. A long black cigarette holder always seemed to be hanging from the corner of his mouth.

I was one of the stunt drivers on the picture for a car chase sequence, but I also got to drive him around and take him home each night to his hotel. We filmed the movie in County Limerick in Ireland and he loved it. We would sit down some nights and he'd become an encyclopedia of wonderful stories. Most of them were very rude and often involving his old pal Richard Harris. One that was relatively clean was an occasion where Peter and Richard had been out frolicking around London town. This he added was many years before fame and fortune. Richard was living in a 'hole' of a flat in Hammersmith and Peter wasn't living anywhere in particular so he decided to kip on what spare floor he could find in Richard's place. When they got in they both decided that they were incredible hungry and raided the freezer only to find one very sorry-looking pork chop. They looked at it and at each other. Then gave it a suspect sniff. They decided it wasn't for them and Richard threw it out of the window.

The following morning, they walked outside and underneath the window where the chop had been thrown lay a dead dog. He added,

"Richard tells it in a slightly different way. He tells everyone it was a dead cat, which just goes to show how drunk he really was."

One other great story was one he told me one night in the hotel. Perhaps it was the feel of being in Ireland that set him off, but he was in fine form. So, he was in Dublin with Peter Finch. They were great mates. Finch was living a few miles outside Dublin and after an evening of 'the usual', they retired back to the Finch residence. On the way back, they spotted a tiny bar, practically a hole in the wall. And what with it being only just after four a.m. they decided to pop in for a few short ones before bed. They had a few drinks and then a few more. The landlord then said, "Righto, lads, that's enough now. You two have had quite enough and I'm not going to serve you any more tonight." As you can imagine Messrs. O'Toole and Finch weren't ready to go so, they bought the bar. As you do!

The following morning Peter says to Peter, "Do you remember what we did last night? Well I'll tell you. We bought the bar next door." So, they went in to see the landlord who hadn't cashed the cheques, in fact he tore them up when we arrived. They became firm pals over the years and about five to six years later they received the terrible news that the barman had passed away. They had become quite friendly with him and his family so went over to Ireland for the funeral. They arrived at the graveside and stood among the grieving family members who wept openly on that cold October morning. A few moments after the service was completed the family members turned and filed past the two Peters. It was only at this point did they realize that they had both been standing at the wrong graveside.

So, filming had ended for us both, but we kept in touch and later that year we had the Annual Stunt Ball at the Grosvenor House Hotel in London. I had invited Peter O'Toole along as my guest. The evening was getting on and still no sign of Peter. Just then, upstairs, I saw him, standing on the balcony looking down, waving at me. He came down to our table. He'd brought his daughter along with him. My mate John Virgo was at our table and it turned out that Peter was a massive snooker fan and a fan of Virgo's. One of the lasting memories I have of that evening is watching his daughter rolling cigarettes and passing them to her dad. Lovely. A truly lovely man who is always missed to this day.

BLAKE EDWARDS

Blake Edwards was a very powerful man. He was a gentleman and he loved to laugh, which is why the Pink Panther series of films had so many outtakes as the cast and crew would break up in fits of laughter during almost every shot.

His stunt coordinator was a great friend of mine called Joe Dunne who had worked with me many years before on *The Avengers* and similar sixties TV projects. Joe was a very funny man too which is why Blake liked to have him around. The two of them got on very well and before too long a story would be told, and everyone had tears rolling down their faces.

Blake came up to me and Eddie Stacey and asked if we would mind getting dressed up as transvestites for a fight scene in the movie *Victor/Victoria*. I looked at Eddie who looked at me and shook his head in disgust. "Mr Edwards, I'm over six feet tall and I'm a hairy bloke... do you really want us to do this?" Blake said he did and that the fight needed a few comedic turns along the way in order to make it work.

I spoke to Eddie for a moment and then went back to Blake. "Mr Edwards we will do this for you, but on one condition."

Blake moved a little closer. "Name it, Rocky," he said, presumably expecting me to say I needed more money.

"I want you to promise me that I'll be the most beautiful man on that set."

He laughed and said, "Sweetheart, I'll make you so beautiful you won't be able to sit down for a week!"

So, there we were Eddie and me in wardrobe going through the outfits. Didn't like this one, couldn't fit in that one, this is too revealing, this one doesn't show enough... eventually we settled on our gowns for the sequence. Once we were made up and looking gorgeous we decided to indulge in a little dinner in the restaurant. We got in just before it opened and sat at a table that made us the centre of attention as the people came in. Well the looks we got were priceless. Eddie said, "They can't take their eyes off us."

I said, "I know. Now I know how women must feel." Admittedly you wouldn't find a woman wearing such a lovely frock with a hairy chest hanging out where the cleavage should be, but still we loved it.

The fight was very good too, plenty of laughs and James Garner really knew how to throw a punch.

I'd worked with Blake before on the Pink Panther pictures and he does possess a real sense of authority. He had hired a plane to take the cast and crew to the location for *The Pink Panther Strikes Again* and he had requested that the plane was pink. He turned up at Heathrow and was taken to the plane which was a very dazzling gold colour. "What is that?" enquired Blake with a stern expression on his face.

"It's your plane, sir," said a young man from the airline.

Blake beckoned to him with a finger. "Why is it gold? Are we making the Gold Panther? No, it's the Pink Panther and the idea that the cast and crew of this movie should turn up on location in a gold plane does seem a little stupid... not to mention unfunny. So, I need a pink aircraft."

The young man scratched his head and tried to talk his way out of it. "We couldn't get a pink one, sir. So we thought that gold would be just as good, if not better because gold is for winners as you will prove with this film... sir."

I'll be honest. For a young man, still wet behind the ears he'd got big balls and Blake realized this and sort of liked his attempt at overcoming this glitch. "Pink by Monday or I find an airline that will get me a pink plane... okay?"

Well, Monday came around, and guess what? Yep on the runway waiting for us was a pink 747. Now that is power.

Blake and Joe created some great action sequences. In *Curse of the Pink Panther* Herbert Lom dives into a swimming pool filled with jelly. This was filmed on the back lot at Pinewood and stuntman Roy Alon would be doubling Mr Lom. I remember watching in horror as Roy bounced on the springboard and sprang ten feet into the air then belly flopped onto the surface of the jelly and never moved. I thought he'd broken his back. I couldn't believe the impact he'd had hitting the surface. "And cut, print." Roy never moved. Then we heard moaning and groaning. Roy was alive and well, his body ached all over and his chest was red raw from his landing but done in the film for comedic effect. I don't think I wanted to try it.

I also did a few bits on *Pink Panther Strikes Again*. I was a very well dressed hit man in Munich with a floppy brimmed hat and blades in my shoes. Then I got to double Peter Sellers at the end of the movie as he is about to get into bed with Lesley Anne Down. He is attacked by Cato and the bed flips up, through the wall and the three of us fall down into a moat about eight feet deep. I know it wasn't deep as I hit the bottom with my bottom.

ALAN STUART

Let me tell you an example of a tricky little gag done at night on the Stanley Kubrick picture *Clockwork Orange.* On the back streets of Shenley, I was asked by Joe Wadham to ride a motorcycle towards an oncoming van down streets with no lights. The street lights were switched off and the only light apart from my headlight on the bike and the headlights of the oncoming van, driven by Alan Stuart incidentally, were the torches in the trees.

I get part way down the road and swerve to avoid the van which sends me towards the hedge where a ramp has been built, but only the base of it has been lit by torchlight. I go up that at fifty m.p.h., over the hedge and into a box rig set the other side. Pretty hairy at night and it's a good job that Alan Stuart didn't have any extra wellie on, otherwise he'd have hit me for real.

Alan is a good man and we've known each other for years. He was on lots of *Sweeneys* with me. He was doing a picture called *Hanover Street* which starred Harrison Ford. In it a motorbike chase is called for and a jump across a ravine is required so that Harrison Ford and Christopher Plummer can escape. In those days you would only bring on boys who were good at motorbikes and on the stunt register for such a jump. "Rocky," says Alan over lunch one day, "can you do this jump for me?"

I looked at the idea and examined the photos taken of the jump site. "No, mate, I wouldn't be comfortable doing it. It's a specialized job, bloody big jump too and even though I know my way around bikes I also know my limitations. So, no it's not for me."

He understood and accepted my decline. Others wouldn't but Alan is a good judge of character and in the end had to bring a specialist in. That specialist was Eddie Kidd who did a brilliant job and then went on to become the biggest motorcycle daredevil the world had ever seen – even Knievel was a fan.

THE MACKINTOSH MAN

I was asked to be involved in this Paul Newman picture which was a great film, directed by John Huston and co-starring James Mason. What an honour. Joe Powell was stunt coordinator and I was there with Marc Boyle: two men known in the business for motorbikes.

I was asked if I could do a particular stunt in the movie and this is how Joe Powell explained it to me. "Rocky, what we need you to do is to ride into the prison yard, pick up a passenger, then ride up the wall over the wall and ride down the other side to safety."

I couldn't believe what I was hearing. It sounded so ridiculous, the idea that a motorbike could ride up a vertical wall some thirty feet and over it was just plain stupid. "So, can you do it, Rocky?"

I looked at him for a moment, almost in disbelief and said, "Well no, but I can do it if we build a wall flat on the ground and just change the camera angles. I can ride over the wall in one direction, then ride back in the other direction and then I'll do a small jump so that in the edit you can have everything you want."

Joe nodded and said, "No, mate, it has to be done for real." I tried to make him understand that I may not be the greatest motorcycle man in the world, but there isn't a man on the planet that could perform that for real. I couldn't understand why I was having to explain this to Joe either, as he was a very competent stuntman who had performed many incredible stunts in his time.

He said, "John Huston says it can be done and he's prepared to bring a guy from the States who says he can do it for the movie."

Well I was open mouthed. "You're talking nonsense, Joe, and so is John Huston, but if he says this fella can do it then I'll pay good money to stand here and watch him do it."

So, this stunt team turned up from the US and spent two weeks on the back lot at Pinewood doing twenty-five-foot ramp jumps and landing on the back wheel. Perhaps they had to get used to the bike, but this jump wasn't going to prepare them for the actual shot.

Three weeks went by and someone said to one of the assistant directors, "Hey where are the Yanks for this motorbike job?"

Just at that moment an airplane was flying over. Quick as you like he looked up and said, "There they go now." Two days later we were told that the stuntman who was to perform the job had fallen down the stairs in the hotel and badly twisted his ankle. Game Over! They'd been over here on a daily rate, hotels, meals, transport etc. knowing full well they were never going to be able to complete the shot successfully. In the end the scene was filmed using a net which takes the prisoners over the wall to waiting motorbikes. Some people really know how to take the piss!

SAVING PEOPLE'S LIVES

An odd title for a chapter I know, but strangely enough it's happened on more than one occasion. I don't make a habit of it, it's more a case of being in the right place at the right time, but still something I thought I should tell you about.

It started on a picture called *Krull* which was a fantasy picture filmed at Pinewood. Dinny Powell is in a dark and dirty pool of water swimming to safety. The leaves, floating on the surface, are made of a thin plastic so they can keep their look throughout the scene. Dinny goes under the water and comes up to start his escape.

Now in the restaurant at the same time was me and Dinny's nephew Greg Powell who was also working on the picture. We were about to have something to eat when the door crashes open and Dinny comes in and falls to the floor. He is absolutely blue: face, lips a horrible colour. "Greg, quick, get a fucking ambulance," I scream as I run over to Dinny. I don't know what to do, but must do something so I bang him on the chest and again and again and again until, finally, he spits out the item that has been causing all the trouble... a plastic leaf. Caught in his windpipe it had stopped any air flow and he was turning a horrible shade of black when it popped free.

Another occasion was once again in the company of Greg... do you see a pattern appearing here? A crane was being put in place on location, on the Sean Connery and Richard Gere movie *First Knight*, and Greg and I were there watching what was going on. It had been raining quite heavily and the supports, buried into the ground, started to slide loose under the wet conditions. Me and Greg watched helplessly as this thing started to go. The crane operator, Toby Tyler, had balls and rode this thing all the way down into the water, some fifty feet below. As soon as it hit the water Greg and I raced into the water hunting for the crane operator. Now I must add at this point that in all this horror and excitement, there was a very humorous moment. Greg set off like a whippet out of the traps. He hurtled across the grass and got to the edge of the water. As he raced towards the edge of the water it was obvious that he wasn't going to stop. He launched himself into the air and adopted the position of an Olympic swimmer diving into the pool. Sadly, what he hadn't catered for was the lack of water in the very spot he was due to come down. He came down like a sack of potatoes. Limited splash, due to limited water. He lay there for a second after the belly flop. Then he stood up and ran into the deeper water. By that time, I'd caught up with him. After going down into the water two- or three-times Greg found him and got him up, but he was missing a leg! As the crane was falling Toby tried to jump clear, but the door on the crane swung shut as he was three quarters of the way out. It trapped his leg and the impact cut it clean off.

Greg shouted at Dinny, his brother, to get a stretcher. Dinny didn't have one to hand so he ran over to the catering table. Tipping it over spilling tea, coffee, sandwiches and biscuits onto the ground, he put the legs up and ran into the water with it. Between them they slid the table under Toby to keep him rigid. They then slid him up the bank and got him over to the ambulance. I dived in searching the dirty black water with my hands trying to find the leg, and would you believe it? There it was. I got back to the surface and chased Greg and poor Toby to the ambulance which was giving him immediate attention. I got to the ambulance and saw that they were working on him. I placed his leg next to him on the stretcher.

I am led to believe that this fella is fit and well, with both legs after an operation to reattach the one he lost in this accident. Speed is of the essence and back then both me and Greg could run a bit.

On the subject of making split-second decisions, I remember an occasion on a picture called *Eye Witness*. Stuntman Cliff Diggins was to drive this car very fast into the back of a stationary vehicle containing stuntwoman Connie Tilton. The preparation for it was a bit Heath Robinson compared to today's technology, but the method chosen to prevent the car from going any further was a pile of rocks. Cliff hit this car so hard it shoved it up and over the rocks and almost down over the edge of a fifty-foot drop.

I could see what was happening and rushed around to the front of the car, pushing it with all my strength. Somehow, I managed to stop it just before it fell over the edge. Do you ever do something during your day and feel invincible? Well, that was my day. I had prevented a car from going over the edge of a cliff by holding it with my bare hands. It's a very strange world if I can stop a car from plummeting to a watery demise, and yet I still can't tear a telephone directory in half!

NORMAN PARKINSON

I was invited to double for Stanley Baker on a BBC production of *Treasure Island* for ten weeks in Tobago. Now when I say double it was more doing the running for him, swimming for him and generally looking after him during the shoot.

This was a nice working environment. Get up, have breakfast, go to work, then come back sit around the round bar and have a few piña coladas, have some dinner and listen to the steel band. Then off to bed and do it all over again the following day. Not a bad way to earn a few quid, really.

We'd been on this particular location for a few weeks and we kept spotting this tall, thin, white man wandering about with a camera. He came over and introduced himself to Stanley who turned to me and said, "Do you know Norman?" I didn't, but it turned out it was that Norman Parkinson, the Queen's photographer. The director got wind of Norman turning up and asked him if he'd like to be the set photographer for the rest of the shoot as we didn't have one.

After the war, Parkinson pioneered fashion shoots in exotic locations at a time when long-haul travel was still in its infancy. Foreign assignments in the fifties took him to India, Australia, Jamaica, Tobago and Haiti. "Take the first right and the second left, the first right, the second left, until I tell you to stop," he would instruct the driver on the first day of a foreign assignment, "until the picture arrives." This is clearly what had happened here. He'd been given a job to get a photograph of a very beautiful girl and found himself in Tobago. This was the west side of the island, but Norman who was described as 'carefully cultivated', had a very unique appearance which invited attention, yet he was a secretive man. For all his humorous charm, he was both touchy and irascible, on one occasion ripping apart with his teeth some colour transparencies of his work! Convinced of his excellence, Parkinson never looked back, leaving his images untouched in their original bags at *Vogue* or to languish in boxes in his damp garage in Twickenham.

There was nothing remotely damp about Tobago and the idea of tucking into 'bangers and mash' in this incredible heat was very mouthwatering indeed.

So, the following week we had a weekend off and Norman invited us all up to his home for sausage and mash and a few glasses of champagne. It turned out that Norman is 'Parkinson Sausages'. He has his own factory where he churns out masses of bangers all over the world. Sausages made from the pigs on his Tobago farm and known as 'Porkinsons' were to be served on silver plates.

So, we took a few coaches up into the mountains on a ten-mile trip to Norman's home. Part way up we came to a stop as in front of us was the mountain wall. The road appeared to go nowhere until one of the guides pushed a concealed button on the side of the mountain and the wall in front of us slid away to reveal a road which we followed inside. It looked like it had come straight out of the pages of a Bond book. I was waiting for a legion of armed guards, dressed in colour-coordinated overalls, to charge out and start a mass finale.

Sadly, on this occasion none of that happened so we parked up and got out. Looking around we realised all of the rock had been carved out. This was on the inside and allowed you just enough of your own imagination to start thinking about how mother nature had made this all possible. The ceiling of the inner cliff was sixty to seventy feet above us and as you would expect the air was cool and refreshing. Certainly, one of the best places to be on the island in this recent tropical heatwave. As we walked down into the mountain another 500 yards or so we come upon a machine churning out sausages. This machine was huge. It ran pretty much all day and night, as the demand for these world-class bangers was massive. Local workers were wrapping and packing the sausages as they got shot out the other end. It was a sort of production line only with one machine and only one belt. It is hard to believe that these sausages are considered by many to be the very best in the world, when they are produced inside a cliff face!

To the left of this machine was a bar and in the middle of the room was a table set for twenty or so people. So, we sat down and enjoyed a fabulous meal and had a really good time. After such a grand meal and with plenty of champagne in me I enquired where to find the toilet. Norman pointed me in the direction of a wall where I pushed a button and, sure enough, it slid to one side to reveal a large room with a toilet, sink and bath. Every square inch of this room was covered in tiles and on those tiles were autographs. Every tile had an autograph on it. Except one.

I saw my chance and wrote, *thanks Norman, best wishes Rocky Taylor.* My autograph is just below that of another visitor to Norman's home: one John Lennon. Imagine that?

Incidentally I was accompanied on this trip by my partner Jenny, who was over the moon at spending time in Tobago in the summertime. I went to work, she sunbathed. Day two I went to work, she sunbathed… and so on and so forth. After the first week the sun got stronger and hotter. I came back one day to discover her lying on the beach… cooking. No not lunch or dinner… she was cooking. In the heat. "I'm okay," said she. So, I knew that in moments like these the boys will also have a story similar to this one. Well, they said that if you sit out in this heat for longer than ten minutes at a time it will burn you quite badly. I walked up to Jenny to prove a point. I took out an egg and cracked it then placed it on her belly. The heat was so intense it started to cook!

RAY WINSTONE THE SEXY BEAST

I worked with Ray on *Sexy Beast* and was employed as an actor and stunt coordinator. I got on very well with him and we are still mates today, but whenever we meet or chat on the phone he'll remind me of the day we had to drill into a bank underwater in our underpants. Not any old pants, either…Y-fronts'!

It just seemed the silliest thing coming to work every day, getting undressed and slipping into these Y-fronts, plunging into the pool and being able to talk to each other due to the communication masks we were wearing. That was another key moment for me because I hadn't been using this mask for long and it was pretty frightening. Again, I keep saying how much fun it was, but it was. When you do what I do for a living being surrounded by your mates is the best thrill. And luckily for me Ray is one of those friends. You could see how much fun we had during the dinner sequence in the Chinese restaurant. We filmed that in Putney and not only was the food very good, but the laughs you see on screen are genuine… we did have a good time.

Also, I remember the occasion when we were waiting for (Sir) Ben Kingsley to arrive on the set. Ray was a bit worried as Ben was working on another picture and was due to turn up that afternoon. Some of the crew said to Ray, "You know you're going to be beaten up by Gandhi on this movie?" But that was the mark of the man. A chameleon who could turn his hand to any character. Unperturbed, Ray threw a party for him at the beach house. Anyway, he arrived. But he arrived in character as

Don Logan. He had the beard and the accent, the attitude. Ray was dumbfounded.

"Bennie," – he called him Bennie the Bolt – "it's me, Ray, what are you doing?" The evening continued, and Ben wouldn't come out of character, which was starting to get on Ray's nerves. Ray had got himself backed into a room with Ben giving him his best long stares and menacing dialogue. Somehow Ray managed to slide backwards and step out of a window, leaving Ben pressed up against the glass. Before too long Ben snapped out of it and burst out laughing. Which did make life a lot simpler.

DIRTY WATER AND DAVE BICKERS

Whilst I was on location in India on *Octopussy* I was Roger Moore's stunt double. One sequence involved Bond being chased through the jungle pursued by the villain on the back of an elephant. Bond swims across a river and gets into a tourist boat taking him to safety. I looked at the water and it looked very unpleasant indeed. So, I put a wetsuit on underneath my costume and stood at the side waiting to go in. On "Action!" in I went and swam as fast as I could to get to the boat. I stretched my arm up for the girl in the boat to help me in and she let out this blood-curdling scream!

I was covered from head to foot in leeches. Just awful and even more complex to get off. You had to burn them off. The things we do for Bond, eh?

Also on location was the stunt engineer genius Dave Bickers. He started life as a world-champion motocross rider. In the streets we were often followed by children, looking for money or just wanting to have some food. One little boy had no legs and was dragging himself along the ground using only his hands. This annoyed me as I thought that there had to be something we could do. So, I went to Bickers and asked him if he could create a wheelchair of some sort to help this little chap get about. He agreed and a few days later called me back to have a look at his handiwork. And what a job. He'd found an old pram and converted it, creating a little chassis and attaching pram wheels at the front and bike wheels at the back.

To say it was a thing of beauty would have been an understatement. And the little boy's face lit up with excitement. Dave Bickers was a truly wonderful guy. He could throw his hand at anything and was one of the warmest men you could ever meet. He'll be sadly missed.

KNIGHTS IN LAS VEGAS

Around the mid-seventies I had joined forces with Nosher Powell who had created the 'Knights in Armour' jousting troop. We would go all over the world jousting, sword fighting and creating a great show for the public. I went to Australia for ten weeks and had a success in every town, if you know what I mean? Anyway, then we went to the US and were due to perform at the Cow Palace which is a huge stadium in California. In fact, the week before the Rolling Stones had been appearing so you can imagine the size of the place. We brought with us our Queen of Light and Beauty, a Miss World by the name of Ann Sidney, who we would bow to before going off down the tilt.

Eddie Stacey who was with us in our troop had suggested to Nosher that he should change one of his approaches down the tilt. He would ride towards his son, Greg, who is now one of the top stunt coordinators working today, raise his lance and give him a body blow which would throw him from the saddle. Eddie suggested using a sword instead of the lance.

So Nosher set off and Greg raised his shield to block the blow, but Nosher's sword bounced off the shield and hit him right in the mouth knocking out many of his teeth. Blood everywhere. Nosher raced to the crowd shouting, "You want blood... you got it!" Unbelievable stuff.

We all went back to the hotel and I started chatting up our Queen of Light and Beauty. All went well and so started a little love affair which lasted about a week. The show, in the meantime, folded, and we were all due to drive back to Los Angeles spend the weekend and fly back on the

Monday. Ann Sidney came up to me and said, "Look, I've got to go to Vegas for a few days, will you come with me?" Well what could I say? Sounded too good to miss. So, she'd hired a convertible Cadillac which I was driving on a beautifully warm day with a Miss World sat next to me.

The only drawback with all of this was that I had ten dollars in my pocket… but we had a few beers on the way and stopped off for a bite to eat and had some fun. We turned up in Vegas and she said, "You see the MGM Grand there on the right? Well that's where we're staying."

I'd only seen it in films and I was going to stay there. So, we went up and unpacked. Then she said she had to go off for a few days. "What am I going to do?" I asked.

"Oh, don't worry just make yourself at home – relax and enjoy yourself." I looked at her and, although thrilled at the chance of 'enjoying myself', I had to mention that I only had ten dollars on me. "Look don't worry about that, just charge everything to the room and stop worrying."

So, there I was sat around the pool, having a drink which I'd signed for, then a meal which I signed for which was all very nice. I didn't even bother going around to explore Vegas as everything I needed was in the hotel. I woke up the following morning, had breakfast and played a round of golf; then she came back in the afternoon, so we went back to the room and had a kiss and a cuddle bit of fun, you know, next thing I know we're off back on the road. She dropped me off at the airport, we said our goodbyes and I caught my flight. And do you know what I found in my pocket? The same ten dollars I started out with in the first place. I did rather well there, I thought.

LION OF THE DESERT

I worked on a picture called *Lion of the Desert* about Omar Muktah. The producer and director was a man called Mustapha Akad. I say was as he was killed years later in a car bomb attack in Israel. I got on all right with him. Anyway, he had to go and see Gaddafi and tell him that the film crew from England were all alcoholics. By that he meant it's what they do. We have a drink society. We come home after a hard day's work and unwind with a glass of wine or a whiskey and dry ginger. In Saudi Arabia they don't.

Now as the production was building a town that could be used when filming was complete, Gaddafi had agreed for two containers of booze to be brought in for the crew. So, every night each member of the crew was allowed to queue up and collect their bottle of vodka or whiskey from the container.

This went on for about two weeks and you must understand the numbers involved here. There were nearly 200 stuntmen on this picture, but not all stayed the distance. We'd lose four one week and three the next, then two would turn up and six more would go.

A thought flashed across my mind. I remember a stuntman called Victor who left the day before. So, after I'd collected my bottle I went back to my room, put on a cowboy hat, different jeans and a moustache from props and joined the back of the queue pretending to be him. Sure enough, I got his whiskey and realized I'd struck onto a cracking idea. I'd pretend to be others and then got some of the other boys to dress up and get a bottle as someone else. Before too long my cabin was full of booze. Outside my cabin was a light and I took it off and wrote 'Rocky's' on the inside of it. So, we had our very own nightclub.

In fact, whilst on this picture I had a little fling with the leading lady. One day she was doing a very emotional scene with this young man and I sat and watched. It choked me up – I was very moved by the scene. As the scene was over I stopped her and wanted to tell her how much I enjoyed it. "Miss Papas, can I say that was wonderful? I really enjoyed that." She was very pleased and asked my name. "Oh, Rocky," I said. "I am one of the stuntmen." Again, she was very kind and off she went.

Cut to three days later and I'm on horseback in the square in character: beard, gun and ammunition slung over my back. The archetypal Arab. Sat opposite me about twenty-five yards away was herself who caught my eye and gave me a little wave. I waved back. She wandered over and tapped me on the leg. I looked down and she said, "Would you like to come to my cabin for dinner tonight? About eight o'clock?" How could I refuse?

So about eight-ish I pop over to her cabin and her staff member opens the door, offers me a glass of wine and cooks a beautiful dinner. Later that night I'm in bed having the time of my life. This went on for about two weeks on location. There I was in ninety-degree heat, sleeping every night in a four-poster bed with air conditioning and all the food and drink I could manage – including Miss Papas. She also liked aubergines and bananas bought fresh every Sunday. Never saw her eat any, though!

When she left I took her bed and put it in my cabin. Then three weeks later I got the elbow, for making too much noise in the club. All the boys rallied round and stood up for me saying that it was as much them as me, but I was ready to go home. Six months in the desert changes you. In fact, I remember walking down Putney high street with my dad, not long after I came back, shaking like a leaf. I'd not seen that many people in one place in six months.

THE DERBY AND THE QUEEN MUM

I had finished *Highlander II*, came back to Blighty and was feeling very well. So, me and a few mates and my new girlfriend Pamela decided we should go to Epsom for the Derby. One of my mates had a box, so we would live the high life for the afternoon. We had a good old time but just before the last race I ran out of English money. You see, I had come back from Argentina and I've not had chance to change any of my dollars for sterling. [Author's note: Back in those days Epsom catered for everything. They knew that hundred and thousands of people would arrive on the course with foreign currency so employed a bank to provide a mobile change bureau allowing anyone to change their currency into pound.]

I wanted to have a bet on the last race so had slipped away from the others to get some change. I get to the change van and the shutter is just coming down. "Hold up, hang on. I need to change some money for the last race. Don't close up they're loading them into the stalls. Let me change this now before the race starts." Nobody was listening inside the van, so I started banging on the roller shutter at the side. "Come on, you bastards, I want to give you my fucking money." Can I also add that by this time in the afternoon I had had one or possibly two too many sherbets and the mouth was on a course all of its own. The brain was functioning pretty well, but the mouth had gone. I opened it and nonsense, swearing and shouting came out.

Behind me an on-course policeman stood and said, "They're closed, come away and stop banging on the van."

A reasonable request, but I hadn't heard him properly what with all my noise and turned to ask him to repeat himself. Only it came out as, "What the fuck did you say?" The words were just out when he slams me up against the van and slaps the cuffs on me. I was really pissed off by now. "What the fuck are you doing? Get these fucking cuffs off me. I'm not a criminal, you know."

The policeman turned me around and just said, "Shut it. The Queen Mother is behind you." Which she was. Not directly behind, not close enough to hear my conversation or even assist me in changing my cash, but close enough to get caught up in a spot of pushing and shoving should it have come to that. Police policy on Derby day is always arrest first and sort it out at the station. Nothing is dealt with on track.

So, I'm in this van on route to Epsom police station. They put a serious armlock on me in order to get me in. And now my shoulder is very painful. We arrive and as I leave the van my mouth is still giving it ten to the dozen. Screaming and shouting. Unbeknown to me I was heard by a policeman upstairs in an office. He looks down and recognizes me. It was Simone's ex-husband's father. He saw me being brought in and realized who I was. Comes down to where it's all kicking off and says to the duty police sergeant, "Go and get yourself a cuppa, mate. I'll deal with this." The duty sergeant went off and he comes into the cell. "Rocky? What are you doing?" I told him, and he decided the best form of defence was attack. He undid the cuffs and ran with me out of the station and into a police car. We drove at speed out of the station, with the blues and twos on, back to the racecourse. Pammy and the others find me just as I'm getting out of the police car.

"Where have you been?"

I was still a bit pissed, much soberer now after my brush with the inside of a police cell, but still pissed off. "Where have I been?" I told them, and they didn't seem too convinced until I mentioned our friendly sergeant. And to think that the Queen Mum nearly caught me mid shout at one of her daughter's policemen. Sorry ma'am.

I would like to say that I am and always have been a great supporter of horse racing. I love the majesty (no pun intended) of each occasion and the humour of racing people.

A couple of racing stories that always amused me include the one where the great flat race jockey Sir Gordon Richards was being asked by a trainer after a race why he had taken his mount all the way around the very wide outside of the track, instead of tight up against the inside rail. Richards replied, "I thought he needed a longer trip."

And secondly the one about the fella who comes home from the pub one Sunday night and goes to bed but talks in his sleep all night long. "Ramona... Ramona...," he repeats over and over again.

In the morning his wife wakes him up and says, "All right you, do you want to tell me who Ramona is?"

The man scratched his head and said, "Oh it's a horse running tomorrow in the three o'clock at Newmarket. I was told to put plenty on it as it can't lose."

The following day he comes home from work and finds all his bags packed in the hall. His wife is standing on the bottom step of the stairs with her arms folded. He says, "Hello, love, why are all my bags packed?"

She took one look at him and announced, "The horse called."

JIM DAVIDSON

I've known Jim Davidson OBE for many years and he's always been there promoting me in some form or other. Name dropping me in TV shows or supporting our charity events. Look, I'll let him tell it.

The best thing about becoming famous is that you can have famous friends. Everybody seems to have friends that suit their status. Elton John is friends with Rod Stewart.

Ben Elton is friends with Ade Edmondson. God knows why, but that's another story.

Policemen have firemen as friends.

Doctors have surgeons as friends.

Footballers have blonde women with fake tans as friends.

I wanted to be a friend of Michael Caine.

I used to sit with him sometimes in Tramp nightclub. I once told him I was going to do a screen test, to be more precise, I told him I wasn't going to go, I couldn't see the point. The producers knew who I was, so why have a film test? I asked the great man.

He said in that Michael Caine voice, "They want to see what you look like on film."

He went on to say that I must look just above the camera, "Not into it, just above it, and don't blink."

I said, "But I don't know the script, I haven't learnt the bit that they sent me."

he said, "Don't worry about that, just look over the top the camera and don't blink, whatever you do, don't blink."

I was persuaded to go. How could I turn down advice given by the man who shot 10,000 Zulus before breakfast?

I arrived at the casting director's office and sat in the waiting room with Kenneth Branagh.

He talked to me about things we could have in common. He said, "Rotten weather."

I was shown into a small studio and stood in front of tiny camera on a tripod. A nice young actress was provided to act out the small scene with me.

Off we went. It went well I think.

I never got the part.

Months later I bumped into Michael Caine again. He said, "How did you get on with the screen test?"

"I didn't get the part."

He looked right at me and said, "You must have fucking blinked."

Great bloke.

Back in the late seventies I was a television star... sort of... so I began to look for famous friends, swiftly ditching my old friends.

I started rehearsing my live show at Shepperton film studios.

It was there I met some interesting people who did indeed became friends.

Denny Laine became a mate; he was part of Paul McCartney's band Wings at the time. He was great fun and his zest for life matched my own. We both had Ferraris, Bentleys and a boat.

Gary Numan became a friend. He had a Ferrari, and a Bentley... He never had a boat... he had an airplane.

During my time at Shepperton I bumped into one of the great characters I've met in my life. His name was Rocky Taylor. Imagine having a name like Rocky? He was the best stuntman in the business and great fun, so he immediately became a target for my friendship. I needn't have done that, we became friends automatically. Rocky was one of those people that were dreadfully confident but didn't show off about it, everything was an understatement as he talked about his famous friends as if they were milkmen instead of gods like Sean Connery.

The women liked Rocky, so it was ideal being his friend, the friend got the ugly one.

When I did my TV show I invited him on to show me how to be a stuntman. It was to be filmed one day around the corner from Shepperton. I had to sit in the car with him while he drove through a wall and a set of barrels. I then had to jump off a building... I shit myself.

Although I have jumped out of airplanes with the Parachute Regiment, I hate heights.

Rocky set the scene for the filming. I would not be landing in a huge net that one sees on the television. Instead, cardboard boxes were stacked up like a homeless person's tower block.

I couldn't do it. Rocky was wonderful. He must of thought that I was a complete dick.

Eventually he persuaded me to do it, after he had altered the jump slightly. I ended up dropping four feet. Rocky, being a great director, made it look as if I've leapt off the Empire State Building.

One night, in Tramp, Rocky confessed to me that he was going on a blind date with supermodel and all-round beauty Jilly Johnson. It turned out he didn't know who she was. Someone else had arranged the date. In fact, that very night, Jilly Johnson was sat at the bar no more than six feet from our table. I pointed her out to Rocky, he nearly fainted.

With that we then put a plan together how he could woo her.

The plan revolved around him borrowing my Ferrari 5.2 BB.

He would pick her up in the car, take her out to dinner, tell her tales of famous friends, and bobs your uncle. What could fail?

The day after the gig I called him. "How did it go?"

He replied, "Not brilliant."

He had picked her up, in the Ferrari, taken out to a lovely restaurant and then went back to her place, or it might be Rock's place, whatever, but instead of wooing her off her feet he proceeded to bore her to death. He left the poor woman at daybreak only to find that somebody had broken into the Ferrari and stolen the CD player.

He did make it up to me though once, and again it was in Tramp nightclub.

I had just split up with a beautiful girl called Janine Andrews. She was well above my pay grade, leaving me slightly miffed.

In walked Rocky with the beautiful Leslie Ash. We sat together. Leslie felt sorry for me as I had been chucked. I suggested she take me to Stringfellows for a drink. We went and gave the paparazzi the impression that we were a couple. Within twelve hours we were.

Leslie was a lovely girl and we had a fun time together.

So, thank you Rocky for that.

Another person introduced me to was another person that would change my life considerably. His name was John Virgo… and the, rest dear reader, is history.

Rocky… I love ya.

'TELL 'EM ABOUT THE HONEY, ROCKY'

I was playing golf with a pro called Kim Dabson. His girlfriend at the time was working for a number of advertising agencies. She was looking for a big, strapping lad to go around the country in costume and promote the benefits of Sugar Puffs. So, she asked Kim and he asked me.

It was a two-man job really. The costume was so constricting that you couldn't really see where you were going. So, Kim would lead me around. It also proved to be quite a frightening. I remember on one occasion some idiot stuck a needle right through the costume which just missed my eye. Really scary. I can honestly say that now I know how the Beatles felt being chased down the streets by thousands of screaming kids. The fab four had girls and I had kids but nevertheless it was, at times, very scary indeed.

The good points always outweigh the bad ones and when you're the honey monster you get treated like royalty. We'd turn up at a hotel and wouldn't get charged for anything. The hotel would ring the local nightclub and we'd go down and do a personal appearance – free drinks all night, girls galore it was the life of Riley. I did the first TV advert with dear Henry Magee and all the live appearances for about two years. What a job. Back in those days sugar was good for you... nowadays a very different story.

Ah, well.

ME AND GOLF

I know it's always a bit of a cliché when people in the entertainment business talk about golf, but it really is the one thing that, sporting wise, I truly adore.

I started playing when I was about twenty-one. I'd always been very sporty and had played in the showbiz football team but had taken to golf as a gentleman's game. It's not full-on frantic like football is, it's leisurely and still very gratifying.

I've had those days, as all golfers have, where they've had the worst day on the course. Couldn't hit the fairway with radar and on those occasions, I've said to myself, "Right that's me done... no more." Then you have those days where you can do nothing wrong. Every tee shot is perfection, every approach shot is absolutely textbook and every putt goes in first time. They are the days that every golfer dreams about and I've found that the only way to get them is to stick with it. I will even go as far to say that a great golf match can be as exciting as having sex! There you go I've said it. Unless you play it, you don't understand it and that's the truth.

Funnily enough it wasn't until my accident when I was forty that I was asked to take part in *Celebrity AM* tournaments. This was because of the press coverage and that I'd become a bit of a local celebrity in the Cobham area. I'd play for the Variety Club and numerous charity events where people would pay money to play against me on the course then we'd have dinner and make a great time of it.

I've met some wonderful people on the golf course too, not only celebrity players but also everyday folk who have great stories and are really genuine people. When I started playing I joined a club in Leatherhead in Surrey and met a bunch of lads who created a thing called 'The Tuesday Boys'. I still play with them today. Oh, and yes, it's an excuse for a 'jolly up' and we do spend as long in the nineteenth hole as we do on the rest of the course, but it's a great time and the fun we have is worth every rainy day.

We don't just play for the fun, you understand. A few quid will change hands when we have a little bet on the card. By that I mean the score card for the game. We might have a £10 bet on the scores of each hole, tot up who won each hole and then pay up or shut up in the bar. I can be found shutting up a lot more since the accident.

I used to play off four when I wasn't working. The sun was out, and the phone would ring. My mate Eddie Stacey would call. "Rocky, fancy a round today?" Off we'd go have a great time. He moved off to the US and then my mate John Virgo, the snooker player, would call me and we'd go off for the day. As with everything in life the more you do it the better you get. Nowadays I'm off a sixteen handicap, but I do still enjoy it.

Here's a story. I was really playing well in the mid-nineties and used to have my clubs provided for me by Calloway. Yes, I was sponsored by a manufacturer. Anyway, when I was on *Titanic,* I rang Calloway and told them I wanted some work done on a five iron. I told the guy I was going to San Diego for some golf in between shooting on the movie. He told me I should go and pick up a new set of clubs. So, I did. I was loving the clubs and couldn't wait to try them back on the courses of the UK. On the way back, we had to go through customs and would you believe it? the dirty bastards took the clubs off me!

Whether in Spain or Portugal we'd go off for the week and play the courses we haven't played before. I remember an occasion here in the UK where we wanted to play a course in Cornwall. Having been reminded by Mr Lynch re this occasion, turns out we were on our way back from a charity dinner for ex England, Leicester, Spurs, Barcelona and BBC sports anchor Gary Lineker, when Kenny's phone rang. It was

Jimmy Tarbuck, who asked him where he was and what he was up to. Jimmy advised Kenny to try Padstow for golf and food. Kenny Lynch is a great mate. He was and still is a very fine singer and comedian. He was on tour back in the sixties with Helen Shapiro who was top of the bill. On that same bill was a little-known band from Liverpool called The Beatles. But can he sing. A voice of velvet and still to this day he takes his little jazz band on tour and belts out some classics. When you've got it you never lose it. Anyway, he had asked me about going to Padstow, and he knows I'm a big fan of Rick Stein so, as soon as I realized we were going, I thought about going to Rick's restaurant in Padstow.

I told the lads who thought it was a good idea. I rang up and asked if we could get a table about seven p.m. Now as you can imagine, it being Rick Stein's place they were fully booked. "Oh, but we've flown all the way here and I've got Kenny Lynch with me," I said.

A long pause at the end of the phone was followed by:

"Sorry who?"

I knew that the voice on the phone was far too young to know or understand who and what Kenny Lynch was. I pushed on "Yeah Kenny Lynch. The TV personality. The singer... he's a big name and has been for years."

The voice asked me to hold on. I held for what seemed like a lifetime and then the young lady came back on the line. "Can you be here for six and we'll find you a table." She may not have had any idea who Kenny was, but Rick did. We thought about bringing Kenny with us everywhere after that as he quite obviously opened doors for us.

Moments like this make it all worthwhile. Having fun with your mates and enjoying the sport. As I said I'm lucky to have many friends who are in the business. And as I mentioned I like to have a sing from time to time. In fact, some would say you wouldn't have to wave money under my nose for me to get up and do a turn. Jimmy Tarbuck knows this this very well and, when I was in Portugal one year, he asked me to get up and sing my theme tune *Delilah*. I get up, the music starts, and I belt out a version that Tom Jones himself would have been very proud of. I was taking my applause when another very fine Liverpudlian comedian, Stan Boardman, steps up and says, "Eh, Rocky, what are you doing?

You're not a singer you're a stuntman. Do us all a favour and chuck yourself out of the fuckin' window, eh?" No wonder the Germans bombed his chip shop!

Incidentally Stan Boardman, as with many boys brought up in Liverpool, wanted to be a footballer when he was a kid. He was always very funny when it came to having a dig at the opposition. For instance, back in the eighties he used to do this joke about Ron Atkinson who was then in charge of United.

'Ron Atkinson fainted in the street the other day. Right in the middle of the city. So, these two girls picked him up and took him into a building society, gave him a cup of tea and brought him round. "Where and I?" says Ron still feeling a bit groggy.

"You're in the Alliance," said one girl.

Ron threw his arms in the air and said, "That's all I need, what happened to the third and fourth divisions?"'

I used to play a great deal of golf at Home Park in Hampton Wick. I was there the night it burnt down and ended up crashing in through the window and saving as many trophies and golfing memorabilia as I could. I was throwing the stuff out of a downstairs window and somebody else was picking it up and taking it to safety. I stayed in there as long as I could before the fire brigade told me to get out as it was getting out of control, but we managed to salvage a great many precious items belonging to the club.

It was a great place for meeting new people. I turned up one day and the old boy behind the bar, Les, says, "Here, Rock, there's a bloke over there in the entertainment business you should go over and introduce yourself."

So, I strolled over and asked him what he did. He said he was a songwriter. "Oh, really what have you written?" I asked.

"I wrote a few that went down quite well. I wrote *Delilah* for Tom Jones and *Last Waltz* for Englebert." This was the legendary Barry Mason who was a songwriting god when Englebert and Tom were on top form. So, we started playing golf each week for four or five years. In fact, he bought John Lennon's house in Esher.

And finally, about golf I must tell you this. Because I played quite often I got a bit of a deal with a club manufacturer.

KENNY LYNCH

I've known Kenny for many years. He was a friend of my dad's, and he knew him through his many movie roles. He was kind enough to say a few words about how we met and why our friendship has lasted so long.

What can you say about Rocky Taylor? He's a friend, a stuntman which is always useful and a man who loves to laugh. I've been lucky that I get to surround myself with friends who love to laugh. When we're on the golf course, that's me, Rocky, Virgo and Rodney Hutton, I very rarely play any decent golf. Do you know why? Because I spend almost all of the time wiping the tears from my eyes watching this lot row! They don't need an excuse. It can be too cold, too early, too dark, too much like hard work... but they love a good barney. I've never seen anyone so devoted to each other row so often, apart from married couples, but when the golf is done they laugh and laugh about everything. We go to bed each night in pain. Seriously after laughing so much.

I met Rocky through his dad Larry. I would find myself down at a coffee shop called 'Le Grande'. We called it 'Phonies' as it was full of out of work actors looking for a break. Larry was an actor, bit part player, but had so many movies to his name. I used to do extra work and walk-on roles and got to know him very well.

A number of years later I had arranged to meet Rocky in there. "See you in a week at Le Grande," he said as he left that last time. Sure enough a few minutes after I turned up, Rocky turned up and had with him a baby. Well I say baby, she was a walker. His eldest Julie. Now I love kids so spent pretty much the rest of the afternoon chatting and playing with

Julie. She did one of those things I love about kids. If they walk anywhere, at a certain age, and can't reach your hand they'll hold onto your leg. Well me and Rocky went outside, and sure enough Julie held onto his leg the whole time. It melted me.

He's a very loyal friend always looking out for you. In fact, I remember on another occasion when I was chatting to a mate of mine, Rocky came racing over, grabbed the guy I was talking to and threatened to take him outside. From where he was in that corner of the room my hand gestures appeared to give the impression I was being leaned on by this guy, but that's Rocky for you. We've had rows in the past about all sorts. He even accused me of pulling a bird he had lined up. "I don't need to pull your birds... I've got me own," I said to him. We laughed about it then and have done so ever since. Also, if I may, I'd like to add a few details about the Rick Stein evening. We had been attending this celebrity dinner for Gary Lineker and one of the auction prizes was three days away, golf, chalet down in Cornwall. I bought it for £1,600 and Rocky put £800 quid in. I told you he was a good sort, didn't I?

Oh, and Rick Stein's place. Terrific food, I mean really very good, but very pricey. Do you know there wasn't a starter on the menu for under £25? We sat on the balcony, drank four bottles of wine, ate our food and put the world to rights. And the bill came to £600, but there is a happy ending. Those lovely people at the restaurant forgot to charge us for the wine. Couldn't help noticing that shortly after this the price of Rick's cookbooks went through the roof.

WENDY

Wendy was my first wife and we met when I was nineteen in a Wimpey Bar. How romantic is that? We walked home that night hand in hand. It was lovely, and we wanted to see more of each other. Well about a month later she told me that she had fallen pregnant. Quite a bombshell for a young man, I can tell you.

I have to say that back then this was all very taboo. Not something that went on in polite society and my dad, bless him, handed me his car keys and told me to go off and get away until all this blew over, but I couldn't. I loved her and wanted to do the right thing. So, I stuck by my guns and Wendy and me got married. I was nineteen, a husband and now a father to Julie.

Quite soon afterwards I got an opportunity to go to Israel and work for three months on a picture called *Judith* with Peter Finch, then I was off to Athens. So, I rang Wendy and said come on out. My mum looked after Julie and Wendy met me in Paris. There were no direct flights to Athens from London at that time, and we had our belated honeymoon.

There was a knock at the door of our room that day. My dad was standing there. "Hello Dad, what's up?"

He reached into his pocket and said, "Hold out your hand." So I did thinking that the accounts department had decided to give me a little cash gift for becoming a father. Not at all. Into my hand he placed a condom. "Be lucky, son, and careful okay?" Well I hadn't seen Wendy for some time and maybe I was a bit over excitable, but the condom split. We laughed about it at the time, but Wendy got pregnant and that's how Simone came to be.

Later on, when the kids had grown up a bit and my dad had moved out to South Africa, we'd moved to Putney and had got onto the council list as we were living in Dad's old house. I was away on a picture and I rang home. Wendy told me that the council had been in touch and were going to convert our house into flats, but they'd asked us to move out into a place in West Hill, Putney. When I came back we had a look and it was spectacular. It was on the top of West Hill in Putney, an extraordinary manor house overlooking the rest of the world and previously occupied by the Lord Mayor. This place was sensational: beautifully decorated, classic interiors. I took one look at it and decided it was the right thing to do.

So, I bought it. Not long afterwards I went off on a production called *The Protectors* with Robert Vaughn and Nyree Dawn Porter and, whilst out filming I met Jenny Lee-Wright. What can I say? I was a naughty boy and I found myself falling in love with her. Wendy found out, which broke my heart because I was the one who was staying out nights and being the arsehole and she didn't deserve that.

I moved in with Jenny and got to see the kids whenever I could. Wendy was working at the hospital in Roehampton as a secretary and one day I got a phone call from my mum telling me that Wendy had been diagnosed with cancer and had been given six months to live.

It destroyed me. I couldn't come to terms with this terrible news. I spent more time with Wendy during that period and I took her down to Whitstable to see her mum as she was having trouble with mobility by this time. What was most shocking was how two people could be so much in love with each other second time around. We had talked about getting back together again once she was feeling better. The time we'd spent together had allowed my past failings to be overlooked and we had given each other the one thing our relationship had been lacking: time. We spent time with each other and our feelings had grown day by day. To see her die so young at thirty-three was just awful and I wouldn't wish that on anyone because I know how painful loss can be. Thank you, Wendy, for everything. Thank you for my two beautiful daughters and my grandchildren. You would be proud of them all as I am. God bless you x

DYSLEXIA

I wasn't an academic at school. I was a practical, physical sort of kid. I loved football and cricket and played for the school with medals and awards to show for it. But when it came to classroom work I was branded a 'dunce'. That was the term people used back in those days to describe what we now know as dyslexia. There are different forms of dyslexia. You can be blind to words or numbers. For me it's always been words. I see them, and I read bits and pieces, but too much text starts to blur together and before long I just can't see the words on the page. You hear people saying that they are 'word blind'. Well that was me. I couldn't understand how people were able to read. I just couldn't do it. It bugged me through my whole life. Especially in this business where you have to read scripts. I would have loved to have been an actor. I'm a card-carrying Equity member and as a member I have to act, but not in the way of Bogart or Cary Grant. That's what I would have loved to have done. But I knew that when I went to an audition I would have to read for the part. Reading terrified me. I really must thank an old stuntman/actor Max Faulkner for getting me over my fear of reading. Max was a very fine actor. He was acting in many TV shows long before he was stunting. He was acting in *I Was Monty's Double* and *Ivanhoe*. Regular shows. He became a bit of a face just like Dad. Max knew Dad and I would go along to Max's place in Kensington on and Monday, Tuesday and Wednesday for an hour and a half. He'd teach me about breathing and understanding words and most importantly remembering the words. Which is why to this day I can perform the soliloquy from

Richard III off the top of my head. If I get a script through these days I get Pammy to read it to me. I can absorb the action and understand the plot with the twists and turns that I'm expected to work on as a stunt coordinator. She then marks off the car stunts or the fight scenes and I can read those sections.

Technology has made my life a lot easier to deal with. I have a mobile like everyone else in the world, but I couldn't send a text to save my life. Not if I had to type in the words. But technology allows me to speak into my phone and the phone types the words on the screen. It's like magic and means that I can keep up with the world around me. Having Siri on my phone has changed the way I communicate with everyone, which works for me.

JUDO

Dad said one day, "I'm going to take you to do judo." I hadn't a clue what that was, but he explained it to me and it sounded like fun. So, he would take me to the judo-kwai which was on Orange Street run by Joe and Doug Robinson, who later went on to be pals of mine in the business. To get a black belt you simply find a good teacher and begin training.

Well with 'the Robinsons' I had the best. No doubt about that. A wide range of serious training partners also helps. They gave me bouts with everyone and anyone in my time there to improve me week by week. But most importantly you must devote yourself to your practice and work hard. It's not easy, but it is a step-by-step training process and some day, who knows when, it may come. It may take a few years, it may take ten years, or you may never achieve it. A candidate for black belt will realize that the belt is not as important as the lessons learned along the way. I used to go three times a week, come down by train, meet my dad for coffee then go off for judo lessons and get the train back home at seven p.m. I did that religiously for two to three years and became a black belt. Now I got very good so much so that Dougie and Joe wanted to get me into the squad for the 1960 Olympics in Rome, but by this time I had discovered birds and my heart wasn't in judo, as much after that. It did give me an enormous sense of pride and purpose. I believe that judo made me a man and I was so proud that my dad invited me into it and it gave me a career.

Also, as a side to this, but I discovered that judo wasn't a recognized sport at the 1960 Olympics and didn't become official until 1964 in

Tokyo, which is a good job as by that time I'd done a number of TV shows and movies and was earning more than I could have ever dreamt. Funny bloody world, isn't it?

RAIDERS OF THE LOST ARK

In the first Indiana Jones adventure I was selected to play the part of a German driver during the famous truck chase. Now as many of you will know, this is the sequence where Indy has a fight in the truck with the driver, is thrown through the windscreen and goes under the truck, climbs back onto the truck and then gets rid of the driver. A very famous stunt sequence and one that made stuntman Terry Leonard a household name overnight.

But what you may not know is that I did all the testing of the stunt before Terry took over. We dug the trench in the road and tested the pipe that had been fitted to the underside of the truck. I then had to get under the truck and drag myself along the length of the truck using the bar we had fitted earlier, then come out the back and try to climb up into the vehicle. Which I must say was very difficult. Terry then came along and took over as double for that sequence. I did double Harrison just leading up to this riding the horse to catch up with the truck, but what a movie to work on. At the time I remember we all sat round on set in Tunisia thinking that this movie was never going to make any money at the box office and yet, when I attended the premiere, I stood and applauded with everyone else. It's a wonderful movie and I was so very lucky to be a part of it.

Also, as you will see from any publicity shots of me in the movie, my hair is blond. Very blond. The initial conversation I had with the hair and make-up girls was that the German soldiers at that time would have had blond hair. Did I want to wear a wig? Well no not really so they bleached my hair a kind of 'Swedish hooker blonde', no offence please to anyone either from Sweden or who is blonde, it was so bright, and to make it worse, my scalp was badly burned from the bleach!

So, I turn up on set. I am to drive the chased car with my old friend Romo Gorrera in the passenger seat. Mickey Moore, the second unit director, looked at me and smiled. In fact, many of the crew smiled as they saw me. Mr Spielberg walked up to me as I sat in the driver's seat waiting to go for the take. He walked along the truck with Frank Marshall, the producer, and was nodding his head, "Good, good, excellent, nice...," he arrived at the door. I turned to look at him. "Okay," he said, "put a hat on, Rocky." He smiled as he turned and walked to the camera car. A hat was quickly brought out. I put it on. "Okay, now we're ready," came Spielberg's voice over the radio. I had to wear a hat for the rest of the shoot.

Shortly after this my daughter Simone and Jenny Lee Wright had come out to Tunisia to celebrate Simone's fifteenth birthday. I must admit at this point that with my blond hair I had become quite susceptible to the sun. I was raw from the sun. I know Simone thought this was very funny, but there really is nothing worse than that: not being able to sleep because your skin is burnt. So, we sat in this lovely restaurant and were toasting Simone's health when who should walk through the door but George Lucas. George recognized me from the filming we'd done a few days before. Difficult not to with this shock of blond hair. "Hi Rocky. What's the occasion?" I stood up and introduced him to Simone, telling him about the birthday celebrations. "A birthday, well you can't celebrate with just one bottle of champagne. Stay there." And with that he went over to the bar. For the rest of the night we ate, drank and had a jolly good time all thanks to George Lucas. He didn't have to do it, but it was an incredibly nice gesture.

MALCOLM ROBERTS

Who I hear you cry? Let me tell you. Malcolm was a friend of mine who I first met when I played football in the Showbiz XI. He was a sensational singer. He began his career in the entertainment industry as an actor and had a small role in *Coronation Street*. His work as Tony in *West Side Story* led to a role in the musical *Maggie May* at the Adelphi Theatre in 1964. He had three huge hits with *Time Alone Will Tell*, *May I Have the Next Dream with You* and *Love Is All* in 1969 and represented Luxembourg in the 1985 Eurovision Song Contest finishing thirteenth. Not only that but he had trials for Manchester City which is why I always thought that showbiz gained, and football lost.

Football was how we met, and we got on very well. We were football mates for years, we'd play golf together or we'd turn up at the same pro-am tour and have a catch-up.

Then cut to years later and I'm sitting in Morton's restaurant in Berkeley Square and this guy walks in with a red leather jacket and blond hair. He turns, looks straight at me and shouts "ROCKY!" It's only Malcolm Roberts. The reason he never became a huge star was that he could never get on with management. He wanted to do everything himself and, although you've got to admire him for that, it's just not practical. Anyway, he used to come up to my flat and we had a laugh and a joke and got on really well. So much so that I would go around with him as his road manager. I'd take him to gigs and make sure the dressing room was all laid out beautifully. Bottle of wine chilled for after or a drop of brandy before going on to keep the tubes free flowing. Look after him, drive him down, get him out after the show and drive him home as a mate. I don't remember getting paid. I did it for friendship and did that for a year or two. I would stand at the back of the theatre in Blackpool where he sang to a packed crowd of applauding and adoring fans listening to his voice. It was beautiful. He then asked me to be his manager. So, I was ringing around trying to book a few dates for him. I got him a few Variety Club functions, but nothing big.

Malcolm had recorded a new song and I passed it on to a record promoter who loved it but wasn't sure what Malcolm wanted to do with it. I was pretty sure he should release it, but who'll sign him up? This promoter said, "Why doesn't he strike a deal with Tesco and Sainsbury's, so he can release his music in store? They're all doing it and you see how many records are being sold these days in supermarkets." I thought it was a brilliant idea. I approached Malcom who hated the idea. "I can't release my music in Tesco… I'm Malcolm Roberts." He didn't see the potential and it affected him badly. Many, many years later in 2003 I was sat at home watching the telly and the news came on 'Malcolm Roberts dies in car park'. I couldn't believe it. He was driving out of a car park around the corner from the social office where he was signing on, had a heart attack and drove into a tree.

His funeral was a huge celebration of his life, all his pals turned out which was very nice. I went with Kenny Lynch and we were very shocked by the whole thing. It hit me hard as I knew him so well and we were mates.

THE PROFESSIONALS

It was a TV show that changed the modern cop genre. CI5 was much more than just a department of the government. They were a law unto themselves. Lewis Collins, Martin Shaw and the great Gordon Jackson. Or as they were known on set 'God the Father, God the Son and God the Holy Ghost'!

Peter Brayham and Frank Henson ran the action side of the show: real locations, real fights, real stunts. They agreed that I'd be a good double for Lew, Lewis Collins. Lewis Collins was a very fine actor. A drummer by trade, but with style and a charm all of his own. He took his fitness very seriously and trained with the Parachute Regiment when preparing for a series. When Roger Moore left the role of Bond we were all convinced that Lewis was the man for the job. He'd have made a great Bond too. I doubled him for many of the episodes. Paul Weston and I took turns towards the end of the show's life.

Martin Shaw was another excellent actor. Famous now for being George Gently and Judge John Deed. Also, for singing in the video to Chris Rea's classic festive hit *Driving Home For, Christmas,* but that's by the by. Frank doubled Martin for some of the trickier shots and many of the really full-on driving jobs. Frank was a great double for Martin. Unless you go half frame by half frame on the DVD, you'd struggle to see who the double was.

Gordon Jackson was a wonderful Scotsman who just loved to work. He could have been asked to read the telephone directory or sell washing detergent. He'd have done both with the same dogged determination.

149

When Lewis and Martin were concerned about the dialogue Gordon would say, "Ochs lads, it's only words, just say them, hit your marks and go home." On those occasions when Cowley got himself into physical trouble he was doubled by Roy Scammell.

Me and Lew became pals and we would often frequent a nearby watering hole after filming. It turned out we'd worked together years before on *Confessions of a Driving Instructor* in the rugby sequence. I'd completely forgotten this until he reminded me. He liked a good laugh and a fool around. He wasn't the first Bodie though. Anthony Andrews who went on to be huge from *Brideshead Revisited* was the original Bodie. But Brian Clemens, the show's creator, thought the chemistry between him and Martin Shaw was lacking something. So, he remembered Lew who had acted opposite Martin in a *New Avengers* episode and the rest is history. The budgets for the show weren't huge and on more than one occasion Gordon, Lew and Martin would have to get rest between set-ups in their own action cars. In fact, Martin and Lew had drawn up a list of places they could get to without being bothered by the public. One day Martin rolls back the seat of his white Ford Escort and has a sleep. He had parked on a residential side street not far from where the filming was taking place. He is awoken by a tap at the window. Looks, but sees nothing, hears tapping again and rolls down the window. He looks down and sees a mop of ginger hair. There he sees a boy, about eight or nine years old. "Are you Doyle off the telly?" says the little fella. "Yeah that's right," replies Martin as he puts his seat back into the upright position. As Martin's face got just above the door frame the kid throws a punch and smacks him right on the nose. He runs off down the street followed by his mates shouting, "I punched Doyle!"

Lew was also a keen practical joker. Being a scouser he couldn't stop himself. Martin has been vegetarian for most of his working life and Lew was very aware that back in 1977 vegetarianism wasn't very well catered for. So, he would get the catering girls to stick bacon in Martin's cheese roll or cook his mushrooms with lard. Things considered unheard of now but at the time just a bit of a laugh.

Once in a while me and Lew would take a trip down the gym to do a bit of circuit training. Nowadays the stunt performer's body is a temple.

Nothing is eaten that hasn't been calorie counted and nothing goes into the diet that hasn't got the maximum energy-giving properties. In our day Lew and I would have fish and chips or a ham cob with a bag of crisps and a Coke. Then work it off during the fight scene or action sequence later that afternoon.

Lew, a fine drummer in his time, he used to work with Paul McCartney's brother Mike in a hairdressing salon. He told me that Mike asked him one day about playing with his brother Paul in a little-known band called The Beatles. Pete Best, the original drummer, was leaving or had left and Lew was asked to jump on the kit. He told Mike that he couldn't do because, "This time next year I'll be on £42 a week." Typical Lewis.

He presented me with my Stuntman Challenge trophy when I won in 1982. He was a lovely guy and someone I hold very dear. When he died in 2013 it was a terrible blow. Not only for those near to Lewis, in particular his wife Michelle and his three boys, but those who had the good fortune to know him for a short period. A short period that stayed with them forever.

THE SWEENEY

Another one of those cop dramas that really struck a chord with the viewing public. I did so many of them in one way or another and the style of fights that were captured on screen was down to Peter Brayham and his ability to take a script and imagine the type of action required. He was regarded so highly by the production crew and rightly so. Such a wonderful man who really knew about punch-ups.

Talk about *The Sweeney* today and people remember the car chases. But the fights were also a massive part of each episode. Nowadays how do villains rob banks? By computer. A bank in London can be drained of all funds by a schoolkid in Tokyo with a computer and a bit of know-how. In 1975 villains used sawn-off shotguns and pickaxe handles. The violence was brutal, but then these were violent men. The script would say on page 58 'Fight between Sweeney and robbers', that was enough for Peter Brayham to shine with a brilliant fight involving many stunt guys, including me and the actors. Both John Thaw and Dennis Waterman were very handy with a punch. Dennis in particular as he boxed quite a bit growing up. In fact, his brother was a decent welterweight champion.

I remember an episode I did where a bank was being robbed. Old style. Stockings over the heads, shooters and proper villainy. Paul Weston, Terry Plummer and Colin Skeaping were the villains. I was one of the Sweeney team sent in to prevent their escape.

A shoot-out takes place and Terry Plummer is shot. Paul Weston makes a run for it and jumps into a car. Takes off up the road. The next shot is me running across the road all guns blazing and Paul slides the car into me. I bounce off the driver's door and roll about on the floor as he drives off again. We'd rehearsed it, so we knew what was going to happen and where. I put on all the pads I thought would be enough for this job. Elbow, knees all good. We go for the take and in I come. BANG straight into Paul's door as he takes off. I start to fall backwards and realize we're a bit further over this time so, as I land, I end up flat on my back right on the edge of the curb. I lay there waiting for the director to shout cut. Eventually he did… seemed like a lifetime. The one part of my body I hadn't put a pad on and I land square on it. Bloody hurt. Looked great on screen, though.

Another very memorable job for me on a *Sweeney* was an episode where actor Bill Murray, the one from *EastEnders* not *Groundhog Day*, is the new driver for Regan and Carter. The episode was called *Stoppo Driver* and I was to crash through the windscreen of a car at the end of a car chase. But I wasn't going to be doing the driving.

Peter Brayham, who also wrote the episode, was to drive the car that was being chased and Bill Murray did the majority of the driving himself in the chase car. Peter found out that he was pretty good behind the wheel and Frank Henson, who was normally in charge of the car chases, was quite happy with his ability. Terry Green was the director and he always wanted the action to be as real as possible. I'd work with Terry years later on *Minder*.

At the end of this chase round Battersea gasworks the villain's car crashes into a wall and the driver is flung out through the windscreen. I discussed the options with Peter and he agreed we should gut the car completely: all the seats out and the steering wheel too. This would give me a chance to get as much propulsion as I could to dive out through the windscreen. To make life a bit easier we had tiny detonators in the corner of the screen. I would trigger the detonators with a hand-held device. It looked really good on screen. As the car hits the wall they cut to the windscreen smashing and me coming through it. Peter was very happy with it and so was I.

PSYCHOMANIA

In 1973 I was put forward for a movie by stunt coordinator Gerry Crampton. *Psychomania* as it was known in Europe, was what we might call a B-Movie, but with a good British cast. George Sanders and Beryl Reid were the stars and Nicky Henson played the leader of a motorcycle gang who make a deal with the devil... yes, I know... and who each commit suicide as an ultimate offering to the dark side.

I was given the role of gang member Hinky and was there primarily to be a professional among the actors. Don Sharp was the director and was very enthusiastic about the action sequences. A few of the boys had done motorcycle riding in the movie: Marc Boyle, Roy Scammell and Jack Cooper. My character would meet his untimely death on what is now called 'Longcross Studios'. Back in 1973 it was Ministry of Defence land and Don Sharp had secured a section of road that we could use for short bursts in between the tanks trundling up and down the road on exercise.

My character, Hinky, was to die in a spectacular crash. I was to drive my motorcycle along the road with actress Ann Michelle on hers into heavy traffic and through the side of a passing articulated lorry. It's a very exciting scene to watch but some people have described it as one of the best motorcycle stunts they've ever seen. I'm going have to burst a few bubbles here. It was exciting, but in a number of takes. Firstly, we drove towards the lorry. Then we had another set-up riding into traffic. Then I got inside the lorry and jumped out onto the road. The side of the lorry had been painted and replaced with balsa wood. Ann Michelle wasn't doubled as such. She was replaced by a dummy which was thrown out of the lorry when I jumped.

Funny though that in all the movies I've done this one is still regarded by many as a classic. At the time you turn up, say the lines and go home. Time can be a bloody funny thing.

THE C WORD

In 2011 I realized that something wasn't right. Do you ever get that? A feeling that whatever you're doing just shouldn't be happening?

With me it was going to the toilet. I was up and down like a two-year-old. Up half a dozen times in the night, if I was on the golf course I'd have to stop on route and find a sccluded stop to have a pee. So, I thought enough is enough and off I went to the doctor who examined my prostate. Not the most dignified examination I've ever had but got to be done. Doctor said it felt swollen, so he gave me some tablets to reduce the swelling. I thought nothing of it, took the tablets for a year or more. Then the trouble come back again. And I didn't want to go through all that again, so I went off to see the doctor again. Very swollen this time and he sends me off to a specialist at the hospital who agreed and sent me for tests. They biopsied the prostate and I went home. Three weeks later I go back to the doctor and he says, "I've got bad news. We took ten biopsies, eight were cancerous and aggressive." To hear the word cancer is bad enough, but to hear the word aggressive alongside it is really concerning.

"I'm going to die then, am I?"

The doctor smiled. "Eventually yes, but hopefully we've caught it early enough to treat it and sort it out." I was prescribed a course of radiotherapy and hormone injections. Luckily for me I'd taken out a private healthcare plan which covered me for private therapy in just such a scenario. So, I had my radiotherapy and hormone injections through October, November and December 2012. Some of the side effects were very unpleasant and I'm not going to list them here but, trust me, it's not great. When I had my initial reading, it was 11.5 which was pretty high and when the treatment was over it was 0.5 which is very good indeed. I'd beaten the big C.

Although I wasn't out of the woods. These side effects were very strange. I'll give you an example of some of the ones I feel comfortable talking about. January through to May I would get what women refer to as 'the vapours'. Menopausal-like symptoms where I'd be fine one minute and sweating buckets the next. Then I discovered I had a limp. I had no idea where this came from and hadn't even made the connection between the radiotherapy and this as a symptom, but that's what it was. And it got to the stage where I could hardly walk upstairs at one point.

This was really scary as I've always been so active that the thought of spending my remaining days crippled and in pain every time I walked anywhere was so difficult to accept. So, I went to see the doctor and he said he'd go away and come up with a plan for recovery. A month or so later I go back, and he tell me he's been in touch with eminent physicians and specialists in oncology who advise forty sessions of two-hour stints in a hyperbaric chamber. Now I've done diving and I know how to equalize, but normally I'm used to getting my feet wet. Eighty hours on dry land seemed odd.

"Where have I got to go, then?" I said.

He looked at me and said, "Chichester." Now he may as well have said Pluto or Venus. Either of those planets would have been closer to get to every day of the weeks for two hours!

When I rang Chichester they told me about a chamber in St Johns Wood which was much easier to get to and I got to take the train. They're lovely people too, really look after you. You go into the chamber which is about the size of a large living room, they lock the doors and start to decompress. They simulate going down forty feet whilst you breathe oxygen through a mask which oxygenates the blood and it does make a big difference. Once I'd finished my week of two hours a day in the chamber I felt very good and the limp goes too. I'm very lucky to have been one of those lucky few who are struck down with a cancer and are able to come out the other side. I've known many people in my life who've been taken due to this illness, sadly for them and their families the science and technology that we have today may have prolonged or even cured many of those who are now no longer with us. Cancer is a life changer and makes you want to live every day to the fullest, because you never know what's around the corner.

That's why this book has been an incredible adventure for me. The idea that I can recollect many great times I've had on location with my friends and family is very special indeed. I am like a child again. Some would say I've always been like a child, but that's just me. I see the adventure in things long before anything is set in stone. Never put anything off until tomorrow. If it feels good, do it. I think that should go inside a fortune cookie really. Very poignant.

CURSE OF THE PINK PANTHER

A question I get asked a lot. Somebody always wants to know how we did many of those exciting action sequences. Well here's one for you. Do you remember *Curse of the Pink Panther*? Okay, I know it wasn't the best of that comedy series, but we put plenty of action into it.

I was doubling the lead, an American actor called Ted Wass. In fact, there used to be a footballer called Ted Wass who played for York in the thirties and I mentioned this to Ted who said, "Yeah I get mistaken for him all the time!" A nice guy. He was to take on the Clouseau franchise after Peter Sellers' death a few years before. That was the plan anyway. I was his double and in a particular sequence we had a car stunt with a difference. The villains are chasing the hero in a runaway taxi. The taxi swerves to miss a vehicle and flips over onto its roof. Gerry Crampton did that part and I took over as it started off down the road on its roof. Now you're probably saying, well, that's been done hundreds of times before. Well yes. But not with both drivers in the vehicle at the same time.

I'll explain. Gerry is sat in the driving seat and turns the car over. Then I get in and sit in a specially designed seat strapped to the roof... now on the ground. Gerry remains in his driving position. On the roof of this car, a Peugeot, are a small set of go-kart wheels that Dave Bickers has attached so that I can steer the car down the road, avoiding traffic, then run up a ramp and turn it over. At this point when the car flips back onto its wheels Gerry then takes over and drives off. It's a great gag to watch but, as with all of these clever stunt sequences, the actual filming took five or six days to shoot… great times though.

I also doubled Ted crashing out of a hotel bedroom window and falling through the roof on a parachute into Clouseau's home. Clouseau was now played by Roger Moore, yes Roger Moore. He was accompanied in this scene by Joanna Lumley. Roger had a whale of a time and so did I, it was great fun to do.

BRITAIN'S GOT TALENT

I was driving along one day with my friend Gerry Toomey, who's a fine film production manager, in Cobham when the phone rang. It was the presenter of my Battersea Power Station jump. She told me that she had moved on to the production side of *Britain's Got Talent* and would I like to be involved in the show?

Now it's not the sort of question you are asked every day out of the blue, but I thought about it for a moment and said, "Well, I could go on stage and sing a song and in the middle of it I could set myself on fire."

A brief pause was followed by whooping and yelling... and then a very excited voice said, "That would be brilliant, Rocky." True to her word he went off and passed the details onto the production team. She came back to me and confirmed that her producers thought this would be an excellent idea. I asked her about expenses. "What do you mean... expenses?" she enquired politely.

"Well," I said, "In order to make this work I need to have a few guys with me. Flammable gel and the fire-retardant gel plus fire-protective clothing that I'd wear underneath my clothing."

Another pause and a clearing of the throat was followed by, "We don't usually pay anyone to appear on the show, Rocky, but you do have the chance of winning £250,000."

I laughed and said, "I know that... you're not paying me. It's expenses... for me to perform this stunt I will require these items." A figure was agreed, and a date was set.

I arrived at the Dominion Theatre to find the floor manager who showed me where to go and wait. We set up as much as we needed on stage, but we still had to fool the judges. You see, for this stunt to work timing is crucial. I can't have flammable gel put on me and then walk out on stage to be introduced to the judges as this extended period would cause the gel to dry out and therefore my trigger, which I have secreted in the palm of my hand, wouldn't ignite the gel causing the flame. You follow me? There had to be a diversion moment. Something to happen causing me to leave the stage and have the gel applied without anyone on the panel or in the audience getting suspicious.

Luckily, I didn't have to worry as the director of the show had arranged for a microphone malfunction. So, after I had a brief chat with Simon Cowell on stage, the director said, "Sorry guys, Rocky, can we ask you to come off stage for a moment as we appear to have a problem with the mic?" I am shown off stage where my team, stuntmen Jim Dowdall and Lloyd Bass, get me gelled up and put my trigger in place in my hand. A few moments go by and then the music starts. *Delilah* by Tom Jones, a firm favorite of mine. I walk out on stage, hit my mark and sing the first line:

"*I saw the light on the night that I passed by her window…*"

Without prompting the audience join in with:

"*DA DA DA DAAAAA DA DA.*"

"*I saw the flickering shadows of love on her blind.*"

At this point I hit the trigger, a spark caused the back of the jacket to burst into flames and I staggered about the stage, then collapsed onto a heap on the floor. The audience and the judges gave out an audible gasp. Jim and Lloyd rushed on with fire extinguishers and put me out. They helped me to my feet and I prepared myself for any questions from the judges.

Simon Cowell spoke first. "Rocky… Did you realize you were on fire?"

I laughed. "Yes, I did, I'm used to it as I'm a film and television stuntman."

Simon threw his arms into the air. "Right I see. David yes or no?"

David Walliams was very clear. "I think Rocky should come back next week."

A huge cheer from the crowd. Alisha Dixon and Amanda Holden both said yes. Simon looked at me and said, "Well done, Rocky... I'm going to say yes too. That's four yeses."

The audience went crazy chanting, "ROCKY ROCKY," repeatedly. What a great feeling. I got into the wings and Ant and Dec were both thrilled for me. It was an amazing thing to do. I sang in front of an audience of 2,500 people... okay, not for long, but I did sing and then went up in flames. Very cool.

A few weeks went by and I get a phone call to go to the London Palladium for something they call, extra days. I arrived and was quickly put into a group of ten people. What we all didn't know was that they had a number of groups of ten. Ten who were successful and ten who weren't and another ten who were and another ten who weren't. We went out on stage and the panel were sat in front of the stage. Not in costume, but in jeans and T-shirts. Amanda Holden came up on stage and said, "Thank you all for coming, guys. We really appreciate you coming down here today. We all loved your performances," I felt myself getting a bit geed up by this. Amanda went on. "Mr Mind-reader?"

He was at the other end of the line. He stepped forward. "You were excellent. And you, Rocky," I bounced forward. "Your singing on fire routine was brilliant." A bead of sweat appeared on my brow. This was very encouraging.

Amanda walked back to a point down stage. "Believe me when I say that this is one of the most difficult decisions we've ever had to make on this show." In hindsight I'm not sure it was, but I wasn't going to tell her that, was I? "So, I have to tell you all that..." Long pause for effect. In fact, in my head I was doing the tense 'Dum dum dum dum...' rhythm. "On this occasion... you haven't been successful and won't be going through to the next round. I'm really sorry but thank you again."

We were directed off the stage and downstairs. By the time we had finished the whole theatre had an eerie silence. We came down a flight of stairs and were met by the panel. As they walked away, I said, "Thank you Simon, good luck with the rest of the show." He said nothing and walked on. I was the last to leave that backstage area and just before I left the Palladium I sang at the top of my voice, "THAT'S LIFE, THAT'S WHAT ALL THE PEOPLE SAY." It echoed round the hallowed stage and auditorium. I can now say that not only did I sing in front of 2,500 people the first time around I also sang at the London Palladium. Bruce Forsyth would have been proud. I can hear him now looking down and saying, "Didn't he do well?"

LOVE AT 30,000 FEET

I met my Pammy through two lovely people at a local pub. John Hewitson and his wife Irene had said to me about this girl Pam who came in and how we'd be a great match. So, we met, had a few beers a meal or two and do you know, they were right? We were great, and we fell in love, which was lovely and quite unexpected for both of us, which made it extra special. Around the time I was taking the pub on Pammy moved in with me.

After about a year of running the pub we went off to see my dad in South Africa and he, Pam and everything was lovely. Apart from the flight out. We went coach and it was a very draining experience. I sat in my dad's front room thinking about this and I decided I was going to marry Pam. I would make her my wife and bring her back to England in style... via an upgrade if I could get one. I rang South African Airways and the call went something like this. "Hello, yes I'm Rocky Taylor and I'm the stunt double for Sean Connery." Why I said that I can't remember, but what harm could it do? "On Friday I'm flying back to England to attend the premiere of *Highlander II* that I'd worked on with Sean in Argentina."

There was a long pause at the end of the line as the lady from the airline took in what I just told her. She said, "I see, and how can I help you, sir?"

"Well," I continued, "I would very much like to get married on the flight home."

There was another long pause and a throat-clearing cough from the other end. She spoke again. "You want to get married on the flight?"

"That's right." I pushed on as time was ticking away. "Well your captain is the captain of a ship. They call them ships, don't they? Airships? Well a plane is just another airship. And at sea people were married by the captain all the time in the days before commercial aircraft." I was very pleased with how it was going, and she hadn't tried to interrupt me which was promising. "So, with that in mind I assumed that the captain of my flight home on Friday would have the same powers and be able to conduct a service during the flight."

I could hear the cogs turning at the end of the line and almost without waiting for me to finish my sentence she said, "Can you give me an hour, Mr Taylor, and I'll get back to you." She rang off and fifty-seven minutes later she was back. "Mr Taylor we've spoken to your pilot." My pilot!? "We managed to get hold of him and he thinks it would be a wonderful idea, in fact he thinks it is a very romantic suggestion and has agreed to marry you both during the flight home on Friday."

Well that went very well. "Just one thing," I added. "I'm in economy, but I suppose we could walk through the cabin to the service?"

The lady from the airline was having none of it. "Oh, don't you worry about that, Mr Taylor. Leave all that to us."

Well I was over the moon. "PAMMY... we're getting married!"

There was a shocked reply from the other room. "We're what!?" I told her all about the airline and how they would be thrilled to marry us. They pulled out all the stops. A car and a camera crew turned up to the house to collect us. The local Johannesburg press were filming us leaving the house. Red carpet to the car, champagne and straight through to the plane, no passports or security nothing. Red carpet from the car to the steps of the aircraft. On board we were upgraded and sat in very spacious and extremely comfortable allocated seats with enough legroom to lie out flat.

Ten minutes into the flight an announcement comes over the intercom for us to visit the flight deck upstairs. We walk onto the flight deck and there is the captain and the first officer both looking at us and nobody is flying the plane, which did alarm me. How does a 747 stay up when nobody is flying it? Anyway, the purser was my best man and the female first officer gave Pam away. We went through the service over the intercom, so the entire plane could hear us say the 'I dos'. We walked around the plane as everyone applauded and congratulated us both, drank champagne all the way home and then the airline presented us with six crystal champagne flutes as a wedding present. Now I ask you, what a service. You don't get that from your cut price airlines, now do you?

There is also a question about legality. Now when I say that I mean about the 'being man and wife in the eyes of the law' as we don't have a marriage certificate and we never registered the marriage at the local council office when we got back, but do you know what? We're happy with that and love each other as a married couple so what's not to like? The fact that the captain of the aircraft flew sixty-five miles out of his way over the water, so he could perform the ceremony is neither here nor there. Me and Pammy are as happy as we can be and that's all that matters to us. Now what I want to know is, does that mean that we are now members of the world-famous mile-high club?

FUNNY STORIES

I was young and a bit naive but had been given a great chance to work in Israel for a few months on the movie *Judith*, starring Sophia Loren, Peter Finch and Jack Hawkins.

Terry Yorke was the stunt arranger and he'd asked my dad, who was also on the picture, if I wanted to come along. On this day I arrived on set, went to wardrobe and was issued with a soldier's uniform, then went to the armourer and was issued with a weapon. These days many documents must be signed, and countersigned before you are allowed anywhere near a weapon. But in 1966 it was a case of calling out your name, they would tick the box next to your name and you would walk away with a weapon and three magazines of ammunition.

So, I walk over with the other actors/soldiers to the trench we are to be in during the firefight. On "Action!" we are to pop up over the top of the trench, give a short followed by a longer burst of machine-gun fire, then return to the trench before doing it all over again until the director shouted "Cut!"

The special effects man was a guy called Cliff Richardson. His son is John Richardson, the man who every filmmaker wanted on their picture in the seventies, eighties and nineties. He's still going strong today creating magic for the Harry Potter Experience. He explained to us about the explosions that would be going off around us and the bullet hits that would be going off at the top of the trench. I was on cloud nine. I couldn't believe that I was doing this and getting paid for it. Anyway, the morning went by and we heard a shout for "LUNCH!" I put my gun down and went off to have my break.

I came back an hour later and couldn't find my gun. I looked everywhere, and it just wasn't to be seen. I heard myself saying, "All right, come on… who moved my gun?"

The other guys all looked at me like I was stupid. One bloke said, "Didn't you take it with you?" A flash of horror crashed into my head. I didn't take it with me… I left it here. Someone in the crew is playing a prank. It has to be.

I thought I should go and see Cliff Richardson and ask him. "Excuse me, sir" – we called everyone sir back then – "did you pick up my gun before lunch?"

He looked at me with an expression of disbelief. "I don't have it and if you're asking me where it is, it means you don't have it and what's more you know where we are, right?" He continued, "We are in Israel filming during the middle of the Israeli-Palestinian conflict. And you have just gifted some lucky bastard a perfectly serviceable machine gun!"

I couldn't believe it. I thought someone was taking the piss by hiding the gun. I never thought a member of a political organization would have crept in under the hedge and taken it. Ever since that fateful day it's been preying on my mind. What doesn't make it any better is that every time I see John Richardson he asks, "Have you found that gun yet, Rocky?"

One night in Rocky's, my club in Cobham, we had a do on. A party every night there, but this involved the usual good times and singalongs as well as a birthday if I remember. Anyway, I had been doing a bit of comparing from behind the bar and had needed to go for a 'Jimmy'. As I got in the loo there was a fella standing at the urinal. I'm happily getting on with the job in hand… so to speak… when this fella lets out a huge sneeze. So violent was this sneeze that it blew out his tooth. One from the front that had been made for him after he'd been involved in some motorbike accident years before. It flew out of his mouth, hit the window and bounced back into the urinal I was peeing into. I'd had a few beers that night and instead of doing the 'pinch and move' maneuver to another urinal I played battleships with this fella's front tooth. He starts going "Oooh heeey aaarrrggghh!" and I'm going "Wwwaaayyy, aaaaahhhhh… left a bit… you'll never get it there… stretch a bit more, eh?"

As I walked out of the toilet I was met with roars of laughter and a round of applause. I thought they were cheering something else. Then the other bloke came out and he got the same treatment. Someone came over to me. "We heard every word, Rock." I wondered how this was possible. I did that thing you do when someone says that. I did the pat down. I had a terrible feeling and sure enough there, in my back pocket, was the microphone from the bar. I wanted to floor to open and swallow me whole. Needless to say, it never happened again.

Terry Richards was one of my mates. In fact, he was one of the biggest. He was six feet, six inches tall and was an ex Irish Guardsman. Anyway, we became great mates and stayed so for over thirty years. We were out one night having a great time. Got back to his and he said I should stay as there was no point going home at this hour. It was late as I remember. About two or three a.m. I decided this was a fine idea and we went inside.

He showed me into a bedroom which had a quite small single bed in it. "Is this me in here, mate?" I said as I was taking off my jacket and trousers.

"Yes," came the reply so I got in and tried to get comfy. I'd turned off the light and was starting to drift off into an alcohol-fuelled coma when Terry got in beside me! "Hold up, what's going on here? Why don't you get into your own bed?" I said trying to move enough to (a) give Terry some space and (b) give myself some space to get out.

"Oh, stop being such an old woman," said Terry as he slipped his arm around my shoulder. So, there we are. Two manly men. Both over six feet tall in a single bed made for a person of about five foot eight. In my head I weighed up the pros and cons of this current situation. After a few seconds I decided that there weren't any pros and tried to move myself a bit further along the wall so that I could slip away quietly, but this wasn't working so I talked myself out of leaving, turned over and thought about getting some sleep.

Terry had other ideas. It all went very quiet and I had assumed that Terry had finally dropped off to sleep. To my horror I felt something hard pushing against my arse. Everything in my entire being cried out inside in silence. It was probably just his arm that had brushed against me, after all we were in a very small bed. Then it happened again, this time with a great deal more force and quite a lot more purpose. I turned around, in the bed. "Oi, you watch yourself, pal, I've heard about you Irish Guardsmen and your wicked ways. Don't start your bollocks with me." In hindsight not the best choice of words I'll admit. Imagine, please, my horror as he tries it again a moment or so later. Only this time he's going for the holy land. I scream out and jump out of the bed after an elbow to the face. He's there killing himself with laughter holding a banana in his right hand. I was so pissed off with him I stormed off and slept on the sofa. I mean you'd feel the same way too, right? He didn't even buy me a drink! What does he take me for?

On another occasion our jousting team had gone on a tour of Australia. Terry and I would room together as you've already read. One night I said, "Look I'm going off to the bar for a beer or two. Do you want to come?"

He was in the kitchen in this self-catering type apartment we had. "No, you go, I'm going to stay and make us a lovely dinner." Sounded terrific and Terry was a very handy cook.

"What's on the menu tonight then, Tel?"

He looked around at the ingredients in the cupboard and announced, with a great deal of confidence, "Spaghetti Bolognese. I'll be down in a bit." It sounded fine by me so off I went to meet the others in the bar. The place we were staying in was called 'Wagga Wagga' and many of its 30,000 population used this bar. There was no sign of Terry after half an hour or an hour. So, I'm sat there minding my own business when all of a sudden, the cowboy-style saloon door crashed open and there is Terry with a pan full of spaghetti in one hand and a wooden spoon in the other. "WHERE THE FUCK HAVE YOU BEEN?" he boomed across the bar. "YOUR DINNER IS STONE COLD. I'M NOT STANDING IN THE KITCHEN ALL DAY FOR YOU, SO YOU CAN SWAN OFF AND DRINK BEER DOWN HERE WITH YOUR MATES!" With that he turned and crashed through the saloon door once more.

You could have heard a boomerang drop in there. Everyone turns to look at me. The bloke next to me says, "Strewth, wouldn't want to get on the wrong side of her."

I said, "Him, he's a him." The expression dropped on his face and he took a good pace to his right.

"Well, whatever you boys get up to is fine in the comfort of your own homes, obviously…" Terry had done me again! Unbelievable.

You also may not believe that we remained friends through the thick and thin. Terry sadly passed away in 2014 and we all miss him terribly.

Also, on this tour we had an issue with our equipment when we got to Canberra. Our next show was to be at the Canberra Cricket Ground, but the night before our lorry had been broken into and all of our equipment had been stolen: lances, swords, shields etc. So, we rock up to the cricket ground and announce that due to this act of theft we would be unable to perform our show. Well, to say that the paid punters were unamused would have been an understatement. Many went off and found broomsticks, dustbin lids, wooden swords. "You can do the show and use these as your weapons. Broomsticks for lances, dustbin lids for shields and these wooden swords for the real thing."

We were shocked, but these guys were very serious. So serious that later that afternoon we went out to a capacity crowd of 16,000 people and gave them the show of their lives. They enjoyed it so much that at the end we received a standing ovation. We rode around the perimeter of the ground time and time again, lapping up the adoration of the crowd. A truly spectacular occasion. Did we ever get the stolen goods back? No, but you know full well that all the stuff was probably flogged for a small price and all the money made from the sale went towards shrimps and barbies!

Terry Richards was easily recognizable in all his film appearances. Tall, blond and built like a brick shithouse. He came with us on *Raiders of the Lost Ark* and very famously played the part of the sword-wielding guard in the market place. Paul Weston and me, have had a fight with Harrison Ford and then the crowd in the marketplace part like the Red Sea moving for Moses. There in the background is Terry all dressed in black and red, throwing his sword about. Harrison looks at him and causally removes his gun and shoots him dead.

It's hilarious and always gets a laugh in cinemas around the world, even to this day. But the story behind how the scene came together is quite entertaining. We filmed a lot of the film in Tunis and North Africa and our director was Stephen Spielberg. A brilliant director but a man who never really took to the idea of eating the local food. So, for the duration of the shoot, Stephen ate food from tins. Tinned meat, tinned fruit, tinned everything. In hindsight it was probably for the best as many members of the crew had eaten the local cuisine or drank the local water and became very ill. So much so that part way through filming on location people were flying home and being replaced. At one time a proper conveyor belt of crew was leaving and then being replaced with fit able-bodied crew, until they got sick then the whole thing started again. Harrison was one of these unlucky few, but being the star of the movie, we couldn't just bundle him off onto a plane. So, he had to struggle on. And boy did he struggle. A friend was asked how he was doing. The friend replied, "As soon as he starts passing anything solid, he can start eating anything solid."

On the morning of the market scene Harrison was in no fit state to indulge in a sword fight with Terry Richards. That's what was originally scripted, and Harrison had learnt a routine. Terry was a big man, but the sword was quite heavy, and he had to make a number of 'showboating' manoeuvres to convince the world he was an expert. The weight of the sword coupled with the hours and hours of preparation and practice had caused Terry's arm to spasm. This left him in dreadful pain when he picked anything up in that hand.

Harrison goes to discuss his options with Spielberg and the conversation wasn't a million miles away from sounding something like this. "Steven, I can't do this sword routine, every time I raise my arms above my head, I lose my balance and I'm also worried about shitting myself in front of all these people."

"Harrison, now you've told me, I'm pretty worried about it to… so what's the answer? Do we have a double to do the sword work for you? I'll speak to Glenn." [Author's note: Glenn is Glenn Randall who was stunt coordinator on the picture.]

Steven hadn't got very far when he turned and said, "Look, just shoot him." Harrison's eyes lit up and a smile came onto his face.

And that is how one of the most iconic scenes came about.

Now, I've done one or two unusual things in my career. But one of the strangest was in London in 1989 when I was stunt coordinating a TV movie called *The Return of Sam McCloud*. Dennis Weaver was the lead. You might remember him from the Steven Spielberg movie *Duel*, where he plays a man persued by a faceless truck driver. Well, his character, McCloud, had been very successful in the US. A number of seasons had been commissioned and then they would indulge in a spin-off from time to time. This one was set in London and pitted McCloud against all manner of villainy which was all provided by yours truly and the stunt team.

During one sequence McCloud was required to ride at full clip across Trafalgar Square with a young lady on behind him. Dennis is a very good horseman and in the original TV series he can be seen riding his horse down streets packed with cars and pedestrians, but over here we had to say no.

Also, Trafalgar Square is a strange place to film as it's always busy, even if you film at four a.m., it's London, it never sleeps. So, I decided that we needed to have a pathway through the crowd that the horse would be quite happy with. But we needed to test it first to make sure it had enough room either side. The plan was to put barriers up either side, but these might have been visible on screen. So, we decided on rope, which was painted in sections to blend in with the background. I got Greg Powell to test the path by putting him on a motorbike and getting him to race through the crowd. It saved having to spook the horse. We got up to speed, I doubled Dennis and Elaine Ford was the double for the actress behind me. We had lots of people running around in front of the camera position to give the feeling of additional speed. As I'm riding by, I hear someone shout, "Excuse me, you can't ride that here!" Which made me laugh when I thought about it. So very British. Nice shot in the movie too. And a bit of history as I am the only person to have ridden a horse through Trafalgar Square.

I also remember a train sequence in that where Dennis Weaver's stunt double, an American guy, was to jump from a train. He was in costume and ready to do a take, when I looked down and noticed that he had spurs on his cowboy boots. "I'd take them off if I were you, they'll make a nasty mess of your leg if you don't land correctly. Plus, the fact at speed and edited, nobody will know you're wearing them anyway."

Well, he was having none of it. "I'll be fine," he said as he got himself ready to leave the train.

I can see him going in slow motion. Holding his hat with one hand and having his other hand to break his fall. The first impact was fine, but the spurs dug into the ground. I said they'd cause a problem. He kind of sprang up in the air and landed face down on the ground. The train was moving at twenty m.p.h., maybe twenty-five when he jumped. He'd landed with such force that the spur had buried itself into the ground at such an angle that his shin was very nearly cut loose from his leg. He was screaming and moaning, but what can you do? Sometimes you just have to listen to what you're being told. He probably has done this type of dismount a number of times before in the US, but not in full wardrobe. Consequently, he was injured and had to miss some of the filming.

I remember taking Simone, my daughter, to The Stuntman restaurant in Kensington which was owned by Eddie Stacey. They had a big open staircase in the restaurant. You know the things you do as a dad to try and impress your kids or make them laugh. Anyway, it was full, and I got up in the middle of dinner to go and have a wee. I don't know what it was, but when I got to the top of the stairs I knew that I was going to have a little fall down them. I'd done many stair-falls and over time you get used to them. I waited for a couple to get to the bottom and down I went, screamed a bit on the way down, caused many people to leave their table and look over the balcony. There I was in a heap at the bottom of the stairs. At the right moment I jumped up, brushed myself off and said, "That's better." I then wandered off to the loo. Everybody burst out laughing and gave me a big clap! Simone, of course, wanted to die with embarrassment!

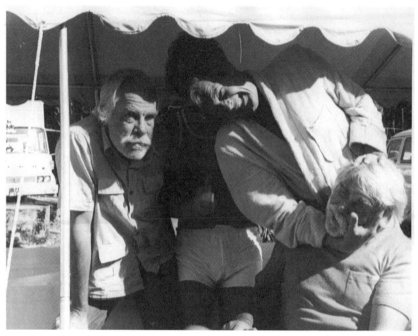

Lee Marvin and his stunt double, Larry Taylor, on the set of the 1976 film *Shout at the Devil*, being 'man handled' by the film's co-star, Roger Moore.

Stuntman 82. L-R: Mike Potter, Nick Gillard, Rocky Taylor, Bill Morgan and Cliff Diggins.

Rocky and Pamela on their wedding day aboard a South African Airways flight from Cape Town to London in 1991.

Rocky with his friends, comedians and golfing pals, Jimmy Tarbuck and Kenny Lynch.

Rocky as one of Stromberg's guards in the 1977 James Bond adventure, *The Spy Who Loved Me*. Seen here alongside fellow stuntman, Jimmy Lodge, and the two leads. The late Sir Roger Moore as 007 and Barbara Bach as his opposite number in the KGB Maior Amasova.

Rocky Taylor winning Stuntman 82. L-R: stuntmen Richard Graydon, Cliff Diggins, Rocky Taylor, presenter Lewis Collins, stuntmen Martin Grace, Eddie Eddon and Mike Potter. Plus, Rocky stands between actor, presenter and friend, Lewis Collins, and stuntman, Martin Grace.

179

On the set of *Pirates of the Caribbean* with fellow stuntmen, Paul Weston and Steve Emmerson.

A picture taken from the set of the 1997 Oscar winning movie, *Titanic*. Rocky plays the character Bert Cartmell, and is seen holding his daughter, Cora, played by actress Alexandrea Owens

Behind the scenes pictures from Stuntman 82.

Rocky playing the character Hinky in the 1973 film, *Psychomania*.

Rocky on the set of the 1982 film, *Give My Regards to Broad Street*, with Paul and Linda McCartney and Gary Kemp from the band, *Spandau Ballet*.

Rocky Taylor in costume, doubling Sean Connery on the 1991 film, *Robin Hood: Prince of Thieves.*

Rocky at dinner with stuntman, Vic Armstrong.

183

Rocky's Guinness World Record certificate, confirming him as the only stuntman to double two Bonds in the same year.

Rocky Taylor and his friend and actor, Peter O'Toole, on the set of *High Spirits* in Ireland in 1988.

Rocky Taylor and fellow stuntman, Eddie Stacey, looking gorgeous for the 1982 Blake Edwards movie, *Victor/Victoria*.

The stunt team, special effects and production crew on Stunt Challenge 85. The competition Rocky was due to take part in but because of his accident on *Death Wish 3*, he was unable to do so.

A publicity shot from 1990, inside the Tower Bridge Hotel.

The following three photos are various letters of recognition from friends and stars in the business. Written around the time of Rocky's accident on *Death Wish 3* and subsequent court case for damages.

Brian Blessed,
C/O Vernon Conway Ltd,
5 Spring Street,
London W2 3RA,
Tel: (01) 262 5506/7.

To. Mr. Ian Mulkis,

33 Furnival Street,
London EC4A 1JQ.

18th March 1990

Dear Mr. Mulkis,

Re: Rocky Taylor -v- London Cannon Films and Others

It was frightful to hear of the injuries that Rocky Taylor sustained on the film 'DEATH WISH III' on June 19th 1985.

Rocky is an artist who I have known since 1963, when I used to spend months training with him, learning the art of Judo under the Robisnson Brothers in Orange Street.

It was already noticeable what a natural, brilliant athlete he was. This, combined with his rather self-efacing, good natured personality augered well for an outstanding future. His Father had already made a name for himself in the movie world, and Rocky was destined to follow in his footsteps.

Over the years, I have worked with him on many film and television productions, his natural althletic prowess augmented by capable acting skill.

Head and shoulders above all this, he displayed an outstanding talent as a stunt artist. His performances in the television stunt competitions were nothing short of miraculous. Inspite of this amazing ability, he never took any silly risks, as is the case with all stunt artists.

Every action they perform is worked out professionally and meticulously. It is quite impossible to concieve that Rocky would have jumped off that flaming building at that particular time if there were not objective dangers outside his control.

He has always struck me as a man of integrity and pure conscience.

Yours Faithfully,

Brian Blessed

ROBERT WAGNER

Mr. Ian Mulkis
Douglas-Mann & Co.
33 Furnival Street
LONDON. EC4A IJQ

April 17, 1990

Dear Mr. Mulkis:

Further to your letter - Rocky Taylor-v-London
Cannon Films and Others - dated February 28th, 1990.

I have indeed known Rocky Taylor for more than
twenty years. In the past I have employed him as a
stuntman and a stunt coordinator in my capacity as an
actor and a producer and found him to be the ultimate
professional; in many instances where he did the stunt
coordination I have, and had no hesitation in doing so,
trusted him with my life.

Rocky Taylor is a fine upstanding human being and
I am happy to make this recommendation on his behalf.

Most sincerely,

RJW:ema

188

ROGER MOORE

c/o Pinewood Studios
Iver Heath, Bucks
SLO ONH

5th March, 1990

Mr. Ian Mulkis
Douglas-Mann & Co.
33 Furnival Street
London
EC4A 1JQ

Dear Mr. Mulkis,

Re: Mr. Rocky Taylor

I have worked with Rocky Taylor on and off over a period of twenty-five years or more. I have both directed him in stunts and done stunts with him and also had him stunt-double for me.

At all times Rocky Taylor was one-hundred percent professional, exceedingly brave, extremely fit and always approached his work with enormous responsibility.

I was extremely sorry at the time when I heard of the injuries Rocky had sustained and my reaction then was that it could not have been an accident of his making.

Yours sincerely,

189

AN AMERICAN WEREWOLF IN LONDON

It was pitched as a modern-day tale of the moon and ended up being a rip-roaring comedy horror. As the title suggested, London was where it was all going to happen. John Landis, the director had been a stuntman in the US and was very keen to make the major action sequence a memorable one.

Piccadilly Circus was to be our home for two nights under the supervision of stunt coordinator Alf Joint, although on the credits of the movie he is referred to as 'Stunt Gaffer'. Another nice Landis touch. On the set we tend to call whoever is in charge 'Guv', short for Guvnor and Gaffer which is another word for someone who's in charge. This amused Landis who started using it himself when referring to Alf.

You've seen the sequence. The werewolf is loose in traffic and we are the drivers or passengers in the traffic. Crashes, falls you name it we did it. I was first asked to crash a motorbike into the side of the double-decker bus as it skidded across the road. Vic Armstrong was driving the bus and the script did require the bus to slide. But buses don't slide unless they are on a skid pan. So, our special stunt engineer, Dave Bickers, said, "Leave it to me, my dear, and I'll see what I can come up with." What he came up with was brilliant. A second set of much smaller wheels, but ones that resembled shopping trolley wheels. On cue Vic would throw the wheel to the right and the back end would come sliding round. Dead easy... when you know how, that is.

That bus also featured me, but the footage was never used in the final edit. I was sat on the top deck with many of my stunt pals: Arthur Howell,

Gareth Milne, Terry Plummer and the director John Landis who rode up there with us.

As the bus slides we act and over act our way through it, but John Landis can be seen hurling himself from one side to the other. Later, he also gets knocked down by Vic Armstrong and crashes through a shop window. He'd got guts and no mistake.

Anyway, a story that recently came back to me was one that involved Terry Walsh. Sadly no longer with us, but a nice guy. He was driving a taxi in the movie and had to 'T-Bone' it. By that I mean that he would drive into the side of it, leaving the cars in a T-type shape. We are about to do a rehearsal as we only have the outer roads closed for a few minutes. Everyone will drive onto the circus and position their vehicle in the right place. Ultimately where they will start and then finish the scene. Once everyone drives on and then crashes, the clean-up must take no longer than a few minutes as the road must then be opened again ready to let the public pass through. So, we are all sat in place. Terry is in his cab and ready to go. Just as he is about to get "Action!" on the rehearsal a couple get into the back of his cab! They said something like "Fulham Broadway please, mate," as Terry gets "Action!" and hits the gas, racing out into fast approaching traffic on the circus. The two passengers scream as Terry brings the cab to a stop inches from the other vehicle. The radio crackles into life. "Very nice, guys, okay back to number one positions, please."

Terry very casually turned and slid back his partition window and said, "That's just £5 please." The couple were so shocked and probably relieved to be alive that they reached into their pockets. Terry put them right as he drove back around and dropped them off in the spot where he had picked them up from, a few moments earlier.

EVITA

I'd worked with Alan Parker before on a movie called *The Commitments*. A hugely entertaining comedy about a Dublin soul band who go from nothing to the big time. *Evita* isn't really a million miles away from being the same movie. My good mate Gerry Toomey was production manager on the movie and rang me one day to say he'd put me forward to Alan and the production as stunt coordinator. I was thrilled as it's always nice when someone you know does that and Gerry has been with me through thick and thin over the years. Anyway, I thanked him and wasn't really expecting much more than that. Until a few days later when I get another call telling me I'm in. Alan remembered me from *The Commitments* and said he'd love to have me aboard.

With that I got packed and left for Buenos Aries two days later. As with any movie you always do what we call a recce first. It gives the heads of each department a better idea of what they have to work with when they get to the location. For me this gives me a chance to look at the surroundings and look at what I can use, this depending on the director's requirement in each location. One scene had Antonio Banderas, who played Che Guevara, singing and then he had to drop to his knees. The street that had been chosen for this shot was cobbled and dropping to your knees was going to hurt. So, I said to Antonio, "You'll need to wear pads for this one, Ant." He let me call him Ant, in fact he insisted on it.

"No, Rocky, they will be seen under my pants." It's best to read that line in a Spanish-type accent... I did try it my own voice, but it doesn't really work. Anyway, I insisted, and he continued to ignore me. Now I like Antonio, but he is a man who is very sure about what he wants and will strive to get that even if it means he will injure himself in the process.

On the take, Antonio got into place. Alan Parker was in place behind the monitor and watching ready to wrap this location and move on. The AD (assistant director) gave the required instructions. "Speed, playback and action!" Antonio walked into shot miming to the backing track, he walked his routine then dropped to his knees. I could see the pain car-crash across his face. I've seen enough pain in my time to tell if someone is actually in pain or not. Antonio was in pain. But he's an actor, you are only going to see what he lets you see. "Cut… one more please, guys," came Alan's instruction. Antonio looked over in my direction. Mouthed the word 'FUCK' and went back to his start position. I watched, waiting to see how much pain he was going to let us see this time. "Oh, just before we go," said Alan Parker. "Antonio can you really drop down hard to your knees this time? I need to see drive and determination."

I smiled and said to myself, "You'll see more than that on this take, Guv, I guarantee it." I knew how Antonio would be screaming inside right about now knowing that he would have to drop down really hard onto his knees. But he's a trooper. So off he went. The playback started and down he came, singing his song then WHACK! Down to his knees.

"Cut, cool well done, guys." Antonio got up, I went over to see him.

"How do you feel now?" He looked at me and I could see that behind the eyes was a child wanting to scream. "Remember this," I said, "next time someone offers you pads… take them, eh?" He nodded and then went back to his trailer, presumably to cry himself to sleep. Which is what he looked like he felt like doing. He is a good actor after all, he might have loved it. We'll never know, I guess.

Whilst on this recce we found a street where one of the confrontations was to take place between the guards on horseback and the revolutionaries. The scene was explained to me and I said, "Sounds good, how about if we put a camera here?" I'm pointing down to a place not too far away from my feet at this point. "The low angle catches the guard's horse rearing, then he swipes down with his sword and slices the revolutionary across the face."

A stunned silence arose from the five or six people surrounding me, Alan Parker was one of them. He coughed, then said, "How about you do the action and I'll work out the camera angles, eh, Rocky?" I wanted the world to open up and swallow me.

The day we shot the sequence I was invited along to the rushes. The rushes are places where everybody from every department goes to watch themselves. Traditionally if you ask hair and make-up people, "How was rushes?" They would say, "Oh wonderful, her hair was beautiful, and the lipstick was just right." Or if you ask the lighting people they'd say, "A bit more shadow on the floor from the window, but we can do that in post." Nobody seems to watch the whole sequence as a whole piece. They just watch themselves and miss the big picture that everyone is trying to tell. The horse reared, the guard drew back his sword and swiped at the man standing next to the horse. Both were Hungarian stunt boys. At the end Mr Parker stood up and turned to me. "Very good, Rocky, great job. Come on everyone, let's give Rocky a round of applause. You were right about the low camera, Rocky. Thanks again."

A MIRACLE ON PINEWOOD ROAD

A few years ago, I received a call from a man who wanted me to be involved in a picture as stunt coordinator. The movie was to be a Mormon-financed production. It wasn't to receive a general release but would go all over the world to the various chapters of the Mormon faith.

I would only be involved in one major sequence, so they sent me a few pages of script. It was to be partly filmed at Shepperton Studios and at the water tank at Pinewood Studios.

We had a storm sequence where the sea was crashing down onto a boat, so they used the wave machine to really make it look choppy. A guy in the boat had to be tossed into the water. All very dramatic stuff. Obviously set in a time before trousers as robes were the order of the day. But before we'd finished we filmed a sequence that just made no sense to me at all. I had to rig the sequence and make sure the actor was safe, but it was a weird one.

Anyway, I went home that day and Pammy asked me how the shoot had gone. "Oh, pretty good really, water all over the place, the waves were huge. Then this boat got thrown about and then a very odd thing happened."

Pammy raised her eyebrows. "Odd?" she said. "In what way?"

I sat down and told her. "Well, this boat comes up to the jetty and this geezer gets out of the boat and walks across the water. For no obvious reason. Didn't really have anything to do with the sequence but I had to work out a way to get him from point A to point B without getting him wet." She was trying not to laugh out loud but couldn't help herself. "What is so funny, might I ask?"

She composed herself for a moment and then went on to tell me. "A geezer? No obvious reason? Rocky think. Why would a man get out of a boat and walk across the water in a religious movie? Because he's Jesus, you twit."

If the production company had sent me the whole script I'd have known that, wouldn't I? I just never put two and two together. You might say it came as a revelation to me.

FRANCHISES

I've been lucky enough to be involved in many big film franchises: Bond, Superman, Indiana Jones. But back in 2001 we embarked on another and this one was pure box office gold. The Harry Potter series had been created by J K Rowling and had been bought as a film option. Lo and behold Warner Brothers had set up shop at Leavesden to film the series. Leavesden was an old airfield, which for many years had been home to Rolls Royce for the creation of helicopter engines. Production and flying stopped in 1991 and James Bond moved in in 1995.

The success of this location as a studio unit gave Warners a chance to have a purpose-built set for the Harry Potter pictures. I must thank Greg Powell for this as he was coordinator on all seven adventures. Yes, I know there were eight films, but the last one was part one and two and we filmed them together as one.

One of my lasting memories of those movies was the cooperation from local authorities. On *Azkaban* they needed a tunnel for our stunt sequence. Liverpool dived in and said we could use the Mersey Tunnel. It's cooperation like that that makes these productions run like clockwork. So successful was the use of the Mersey Tunnel that we went back again for *Fast and Furious 6* to do the car turn-overs. I suppose movies like these are our modern-day equivalent of those huge films of the forties and fifties such as *Spartacus, Ben Hur* or even *Gone with The Wind.*

More importantly from the performers' point of few many of these movies are filmed here in the UK which is so important. I didn't work on the *Star Wars* pictures but I can understand why so many stunt guys and girls were so excited to be asked to be part of the recent adventures. To say to someone that you worked on a big-budget successful movie is always a thrill. When I was in the newspapers after my accident I was referred to as 'BOND FILM STUNTMAN', which is very gratifying.

Now with the success of Harry Potter and more importantly its tour at Leavesden Studios every performer who took part in the movies has a wand with their name on it. Everyone who worked on the picture has a physical record that can be seen by everyone. It's a great honour.

MICHAEL COLLINS

This was a biopic of the Irish patriot and revolutionary played by Liam Neeson. Greg Powell was the stunt coordinator and I had been given a role of a mill worker. I'd be working away, moving bags of flour from one place to another. Then the door is kicked in and stuntman Graeme Crowther stands there holding a shotgun. I turn to get away and he shoots me in the back.

We got into positions after a run-through and went for a take. I hear the shot and react, but it's not quite what the director Neil Jordon was looking for, as I may have taken a bit too long to die, so we go for another. The door gets kicked in, Graeme fires and I crash to the floor moaning and groaning in agony. Neil Jordon turns to Greg Powell, who is sitting next to him and says, "Is he going to die any time soon?"

They shout "Cut!" and Greg comes over, he crouches down to ask me why I'm trying to give an Oscar-winning portrayal of a dying man, when he sees that I am actually in pain. I had many layers on: overcoat, a smock, a T-shirt and a vest. Lifting my shirt, he sees a hole with blood pouring from it and in this hole was a four-inch piece of wadding that had been fired from the shotgun and lodged in my back. Again, Gerry Toomey came to my rescue and said to Neil Jordon, "We should pay him another week's wages and let him stay in Liam Neeson's room." I did and was looked after.

ROUGH CUT

This was a Burt Reynolds' movie that we did back in 1980. I was involved in a car chase sequence in Holland, around the airport at Schiphol Amsterdam and the surrounding countryside.

I was playing the part of a policeman chasing the two leads, Burt and Lesley-Anne Down. More on her later, as they attempt to evade the authorities after a jewellery heist.

There is a camera in a helicopter which is keeping up with us and an additional camera car. I'm following an American stuntwoman doubling Lesley-Anne Down as her character is behind the wheel. We weave back and forth missing oncoming traffic, then a long right hander, quite sharp as I can't see what's around the bend. No sooner had I got around I see the car I'm chasing brake sharply and veer right. I slam my anchors on and steer left to avoid her. If I had kept going at the speed I was travelling at, I'd have ploughed into the back of her. Having turned when the back end of my car started to snake, the back end is now whipping left and right.

I could see the oncoming tree and again made a desperate attempt to sail on by it, probably gave it a glancing blow and ended up on an embankment. Back end facing down, me looking up to the top. I have my foot on the brake and the handbrake on, but the car is still sliding backwards. What I should say at this point is that at the bottom of this embankment is a dyke. One of the many canals that run the length of the country. The car slides faster and faster. Then SPLASH! In we go. I think to myself about how my day isn't getting any better as I cut myself shaving that morning too. I've nowhere to go but out, so I wind down the window climb out onto the bonnet, then the water laps onto the bonnet so I step up onto the roof. I was mortified. If anyone could see me it would have been the most comical sight. A policeman standing on the roof of a sinking car. Then I remembered that the chopper was in the sky. I could wave at it and it could send a rescue vehicle or even swoop down and pick me up?

Not a chance, the chopper flew over... I waved... they waved back... it flew on! Bloody pilots! It was a good hour before somebody came back to get me. By this time, I was wet and cold as the water got to me way before they got to me.

This movie also brought the best out of the other members of the stunt crew. One day I was given a radio. "Okay Rock, take this and walk into the street there. We're doing a rooftop POV (point of view) shot and in the film Burt's character is going to be watching you, the suspect, and following your every move." I thought this was excellent, not only was I getting plenty of driving work on the picture, but now I was playing a part. So, I took the radio and they put an earpiece in, so I didn't have to keep picking up the radio. This shot would take a while from various angles, so they'd ask me to walk this way, then that way, so they got as much footage as possible. Over the earpiece I hear, "Rocky, get on that tram and we'll pick you up as you get off at the next stop," I got on and did as I was told. The tram comes to a stop a few minutes later. I hear, "No, not this stop... stay on... stay on, we've got you covered from another vantage point." So, I stay on. The tram goes for what seems like a lifetime. I get off. Then I hear, "Walk straight on and left at the next junction," I do this and walk down a long road. I've been walking a while when I hear, "Turn right!" but it's a straight road, I can't turn right.

I pull the radio out and take out the earpiece. "I can't turn right or left, it's a straight road. Where are you?"

Radio noise was followed by the click of a response. "We're in the bar at the hotel... see you later." All I heard before the radio clicked off was an uproar of laughter.

I shook my head and muttered, "You bastards," under my breath before embarking on the long trip back to the hotel.

Now you remember I mentioned Lesley-Anne Down? Well I'd worked with her a few years earlier on *The Pink Panther Strikes Again* and she arrived on this movie fresh from a run of hit films. One was *The First Great Train Robbery*, with Sean Connery and the other was *Hanover Street* with Harrison Ford. I thought she was very beautiful and one day, while I was in hair and make-up, I got chatting to a very good friend of hers. Elaine was one of the hairdressers and had done Lesley's hair for years. So, I asked Elaine to ask Lesley if I could take her out for dinner. A few days went by and the response came back. She'd be delighted. A date was set and all day I was very excited about the prospect of taking her out.

Bath, shave, all me best clobber on. I looked in the mirror one final time before leaving the room. I looked good. How could she refuse me? Just as I am about to close the door of the room, the phone rings. I go back inside and answer it. It's Elaine. "Rocky, sorry it's me. Look, Lesley wanted me to call and apologize. She can't go out with you tonight as Burt is taking her out."

I put the phone down and shook my head. "Miserable bloody Yank," I said to myself. Then thought. If I'm being stood up by this beautiful woman for Burt Reynolds that means I was way up on the pecking list. "Okay Burt," I said. "You win." With my new-found confidence I strolled off to the bar to meet some of the other boys.

REMEMBER A CHARITY

There I am one day, sat at home when the phone rings. A voice on the phone explains to me that she is calling on behalf of a charity who would like to talk to me about making a will. You've probably had a similar phone call yourself. If it's not somebody trying to sell you something, it's some call regarding getting your money back from the banks. Anyway, I was just about to hang up when I heard the young lady say it was about me fronting a campaign about making a will. Well, I was intrigued. The idea was that this organization, Remember A Charity, were promoting the benefits of leaving a will and giving you information about providing financial support for charitable organizations up and down the country. The figures spoke for themselves. Seventy-four percent of the public gave to charitable organizations but only seven percent left money to charity in a will.

"Why me?" I asked. I was told that as a stuntman I'd probably got a will in place already, but many people won't have one at all. So, if I could promote this it would be very beneficial. As it turns out I hadn't looked at mine or Pammy's wills for some time, so it gave us a chance to rethink our future.

But how was I going to promote this to the general public? The voice on the phone said we should meet and discuss a few options. We did meet some weeks later and they wanted to use a few factors to make this campaign very exciting. "Can you come up with a stunt?" they asked.

I thought about it for about ten seconds. "I come up with stunts all the time. We could work something out." Before too long I had a great idea. I would create the biggest stunt anyone had ever seen: boat chases, explosions, you name it we'd have it.

They then reminded me that this budget wasn't going to cover anything of that scale. So, we shelved that one. They then said, "Why not recreate your fall on *Death Wish III*? Only this time without the injuries." It sounded like a brilliant idea. The accident that caused me to have this life and death experience. The very occasion when I should have had my will in order. I get a chance to do it again, nail the stunt and promote will writing to a huge audience. We got the balls of action into motion.

We needed a location and where better that Battersea Power Station? An iconic location visible from the heart of the city of London. A date was set, and the promotional wheels went into action. It was to be screen live on Facebook too. This was all very new to me. Whenever I'd try to use technology like this it would usually cause the computer to break. So, it was good to know that they had every confidence in the technology to secure the worldwide audience.

They used the tag line, 'No one understands the importance of a will more than a stuntman.' Which is very apt. Whilst in Battersea I visited Battersea Dogs Home and got a chance to see all the dogs. I love dogs, so this was a great thrill. They even named a dog after me. I wonder how 'Rocky' is getting on? I went everywhere on a whirlwind tour of the country promoting this event. I remember the announcement at the Prince Charles Cinema in London one afternoon. I had to make a 'smashing' entrance to surprise the gathered press outside. So as soon as I was given my cue I crashed through the main entrance of the cinema out into the street. It went very well, and I was particularly happy to see that outside the cinema was my name in big letters. 'ROCKY TAYLOR – ONE LEGACY'. My dad would have been very proud. The charity had created a great short film about me, my career and how together we can make a difference to charity donations. It was a very moving experience and extremely gratifying.

A short while later I was on the *Chris Evans Breakfast Show* on BBC Radio 2. He has a slot where he interviews someone he doesn't know. Well on this occasion that someone was me. The charity's goal was to get a further four percent of the public to leave similar gifts which would raise an additional one billion a year for good causes, which is a phenomenal amount of money. Couldn't pass that up.

The Facebook page for this event allowed the public to vote on how they wanted the sequence to end. Isn't that a little worrying? As far as I was concerned it couldn't end any worse than the last time I did it, right? So, a tower was erected, and a substantial box rig was constructed under the watchful eye of stuntman Jim Dowdall and a number of stunt guys who came along to help out. To build the box rig would mean folding all the boxes in a particular way so they would cushion my fall when I hit them.

The day arrived, and I was nervous. But that's always a good thing. If I didn't have any nerves, then I'd be nervous. If you see what I mean. A crowd arrived including many friends and family and the world's press. Plus, those millions of people watching live online. I was interviewed by the host of the live show and then started the walk up the tower to the take-off point. I was aware that there would be a countdown from ten to one before the explosion was triggered and I jump. I'm still walking up the stairs when I hear the countdown. Not only started but they are at seven... I picked up my pace a bit to get to the top. Walked out onto the platform at the top to hear the crowd and the countdown chanting, "Four... three... two... one..." The explosion went off and so did I. I went into the boxes and went down inside the rig. Nice safe landing. I now had to sit tight until Jim and the boys came in to get me out. It was a very satisfying job. I emerged from the box rig to cheers from the crowd. Certainly, a day I won't forget in a hurry.

The success of this event was extraordinary, and it was televised and shown all over the world. To capitalize on this the charity wanted to top that with another stunt. To push the envelope a bit more we came up with a double whammy. Not only could we perform another very exciting stunt, but we could also create a piece of history at the same time. The James Bond movie *Die Another Day* contains a sequence where a glass floor smashes and the stunt doubles crash through it. At the time this was the biggest pane of glass ever smashed on the screen. So, we decided to break a bigger one, but with a twist. In fact, with a roll.

We decided that the biggest sheet of glass should be smashed with a car crashing through it. The venue this time was the O2 Arena and, to make sure the car went through the glass, a ramp was constructed. A pipe ramp to be exact. I was to drive at the ramp at thirty to forty m.p.h. A kicker on the end of the ramp flips the car over and through the massive sheet of glass. The landing area is a line of parked cars. Again, Facebook and the TV cameras were there to capture the action. Friends and family held their breath as I approached the ramp. I hit it in just the right place and sailed through the glass. I saw the world turn over and the parked car landing coming up.

Funnily enough the biggest jolt I got was when the car came down to rest for the final time. I was wearing a racing harness, so I wasn't going anywhere, but as the back of the car landed on the cars below the jolt went the length of the car and flung the driver's door wide open. The watching world could see me sat inside my roll cage and my racing car seat. I gave thumbs up and the boys came in to get me out.

Soon after I was reunited with my family and interviewed for Facebook and the charity. We had an independent adjudicator from the Guinness Book of Records there to watch the event. After some deliberation it was confirmed that we had broken the previous world record held by the team from the James Bond movie. It was a great thrill. I was presented with a certificate and the smile on my face said it all. This campaign to promote will writing had gone out to millions of people all over the country and had given charities an opportunity of receiving much needed additional funding. So, take it from me. Writing a will is very important. Leaving a sum of money to a charity of your choice in your will, will make a difference. So, go on. What are you waiting for?

Finish the book first… obviously.

CROMWELL

Back in 1970 I was off to Spain to film *Cromwell*. A big, lavish production to tell the story of Oliver Cromwell and the outbreak of civil war. A cast you wouldn't believe and lots of horses to ride. We didn't do any of the horse falls as the Spanish stunt boys would have been in charge of that. Gerry Crampton was in charge of the action and me and Les Crawford were staying in this hotel just outside Bilbao. We came back through Bilbao town and, after a few drinks in a bar, I brought two girls back to the hotel.

We used to get a six a.m. call each day so the following morning I brought these two lovelies down to the foyer and into a taxi. I got back upstairs and received a note under my door a few minutes later which simply said, 'Mr Taylor Concierge'. I went down, and the concierge was most unamused. "Mr Taylor, did I see you walking out with two young ladies this morning?"

I nodded. "Yes, I did. Why?"

He took a few steps towards me. "Because we are a family establishment and we do not wish to have those kinds of young ladies in our hotel."

Just then Gerry Crampton came down and took me to one side. "What is going on here?" he said. "I hear you brought a couple of birds home last night."

I couldn't lie to him. "Yes Gerry, but I put them in a cab this morning."

Gerry shook his head. "You realize the hotel want you out? Yes out. They know why you're here, but if this gets back to the production office, you'll get sent home."

I was very apologetic, "Gerry really no harm done, in any case why me? Les knew too."

Gerry came in close to my ear, "Yeah he might have known, but he wasn't caught red handed with them, was he? Now I've got to go and sweet talk the manager, so he doesn't report you, me and the entire production. Just go back to your room, eh?"

I slithered back upstairs. That cheeky bastard Crawford had done me up like a kipper. He knew full well one of those girls was for him and he still ratted on me.

MARLENE HOWELL

Marlene was my partner from 1979 to 1985. Here she speaks candidly about the time we had together and her take on the events surrounding my accident and subsequent court case.

'Through my modelling agency, in November 1979, I managed to secure a month's work on Flash Gordon at Shepperton Studios. My job was to parade around the set with eleven other girls, dressed in different-colored bikinis. We were Ming the Merciless's Concubines, shouting, "Hail Ming, Hail Ruler of the Universe!" It was fun, and we were on set with Timothy Dalton, Brian Blessed, Sam Jones, Max Von Syndow and Ornella Muti. Many days were spent waiting around the set and, during this time, the girls were chatted to by the stunt boys and the production team.

'I met Rocky Taylor during these rest times on set. He was dressed in a red body suit and looked like a Red Devil! Over the days, he would send red roses, messages and telegrams to me on the set. After the month was up, Dino De Laurentis asked me if I would like to stay on the film as a Hawk Woman, which I happily accepted. I had to wear enormous fiberglass wings and a long gold/black dress. Very uncomfortable and you couldn't sit down in the wings, so the day was spent leaning against walls when we weren't part of the action with Brian Blessed. At this time Sam Jones had left the production under auspicious circumstances and Rocky had taken over his role as body double and was wearing a full latex face mask of Sam Jones, but it wasn't until my friend Camilla fainted in her huge wings on set one day that I realized that Rocky was a *very special person. He was doing a fight scene with Timothy Dalton on a black hole filled with rubber daggers when suddenly Camilla hit the floor. Rocky jumped off the black hole and put his arms under her wings and carried her off to her dressing room. She was recovering and very appreciative of Rocky. He called to our dressing room later to see how she was. I realized what a good person he was.*

'Soon after this we went on our first date to the Intercontinental Hotel, where he decided to shock me by falling down the staircase at the entrance. I rushed over to him, he winked, jumped up and carried me into the restaurant! I was speechless.

'Soon after the end of filming Rocky landed the Global Holiday commercial, which was to be shot in Malta.' [Author's note – Global Holidays were a big-sized company in the seventies and they had many TV commercials. Mine was typically exciting. Filmed on the backlot at Elstree, I was to ride a motorcycle and then jump through a ring of fire, come to a stop on my mark and deliver the following dialogue to the camera. "In my job as a movie stuntman I take risks, but one thing I wouldn't take a risk with is my holiday. That's why I choose Global." They then had shots of Marlene and me enjoying the sights and sounds of beautiful Malta. By the pool, on the beach, walking hand in hand through the town… that sort of thing. Simple enough you'd think? But I couldn't get the 'th' sound out of my mouth. I kept saying 'fer' instead. Then when they aired the commercial I'd been dubbed!"]

He'd asked me if I wanted to come out with him and appear in the commercial. We did this and had five lovely days together.

We did work together whenever it was possible. We worked together on an episode of Hart to Hart. *Rocky was doubling for Robert Wagner and during the sequence I sat in as a double for Stephanie Powers. It was a car sequence, where I had to lean over the unconscious body of Robert Wagner (Rocky) and try to put on the brakes before we hurtled off the cliff edge! We were filming on bricks in a garage in our Athens hotel! During the day we hung out with Alan Lake, who was playing a taxi driver, Jeremy Brett and Burt Kwok. In the evening we would all gather for drinks and dinner. It was great fun. Then from Athens we all flew down to Rhodes to do another episode of* Hart to Hart *with Leslie Ash.*

210

[Author's note: That reminds me that Robert Wagner's usual studio double was a guy called Greg Barnett. Lovely fella. He was very fit and kept himself very clean, spiritually and physically. He was into health food and lots of fitness regimes. During his time on location he was ill a lot. Maybe it was the food, or just his healthy lifestyle, but we used to say to him, "Come out with us, Greg. We're going for a few pints, then dinner, lots of bread and oil and then off for a dance and a few cocktails." We were always right as ninepence the following day. Poor old Greg was suffering a bit.]

THE ONLY WAY IS UP

As you may have begun to suspect I don't have a problem with heights, from playing on roofs as a child to being a stuntman in films. But every once in a while, you should really take a step back and reassess your options.

I was home one day back in the sixties when the phone rang. I had joined an agency called HEP a little while before, run by an old stuntman called Frank Howard. Well, I was told about a stunt that was to be shot in the Edgeware Road. No stunt coordinator just a stuntman required. Turns out that they needed a stuntman to climb down the outside of the building. I was racking my brain to try and remember what the buildings looked like at that end of the Edgeware Road and I'd convinced myself that they were six or seven storeys high. Mostly residential as I remembered.

I get there to discover a building twenty storeys high. I gulped one of those comedy gulps when you realize you may have bitten off a bit too much. I genuinely don't know what I thought was going to happen. I remember getting up there and the wind being so severe you could barely stand up. These were balconies of apartments. People actually lived here. Let's say they wanted to nip out onto the balcony for a smoke? Well, the wind being so strong they could easily end up doing a Mary Poppins over London's skyline.

The balconies were the same width apart all the way down so on "Action!" I started to climb out and steadily manoeuvre myself down the building. I will say at this point that you must never underestimate what perspective can do to your bottle. From the ground looking up you are enthusiastic about what you have to do. But from the top looking down you are starting to doubt your own ability. Particularly in a wind this severe. Once I'd got a rhythm going the building didn't seem so bad after all. I was a bit concerned that I couldn't hear anyone shouting "Cut!" so I just kept on climbing down. Having said that, a bloke at the top did say, "Now just take your time," which has always struck me as being a very stupid thing to say. Of course, I'm going to take my time. It's not a race. I am also very aware of the overworked phrase that has never left me on any high job: 'It's not the fall that kills, it's the sudden stop at the bottom'.

This climb continued for another thirty minutes or so and the height coupled with the wind started to do strange things to me. I had to stop a few times on the way down as I was beginning to see myself as a King Kong sort of character clambering about outside the Empire State Building. Fending off fighter planes with one hand whilst trying not to squeeze Fay Wray to death with the other. When I got down to the last balcony I could see a good group of people had gathered at the bottom. I jumped down onto the ground next to them from a wall and was greeted with cheering and applause. They thought this was wonderful. I thought it was just another thing I could do. Oddly enough some years later I had another rather unusual experience at great height.

Terry Yorke was the stunt coordinator on a movie in India. For the life of me I can't remember the name of the movie, but I'd done some motorcycle riding in it where I'd ridden the bike up a flight of steps at the front of the building and through the lobby, as I remember. Then came this piece of action in a tall office building. The routine goes like this. A fight in the office goes outside onto the balcony. Remember this is a huge office block about 200 feet high. I am attached to a wire and, at the given point in the fight, I am thrown over the balcony and left dangling above the streets below. The key to this scene working was me grabbing that balcony just as the rope took my body weight. Nowadays they have wire work every five minutes but, back then, and I'm guessing it would have been mid-seventies this would have been state of the art.

ROMO

Romo Gorrara was my pal. And as such he deserves his own chapter. We had lots of laughs in the old days and continued to do so till the day he left us. When I started on *The Avengers* I was told to go up to the wardrobe department to meet the other stunt boys: Terry Richards, Terry Plummer, Les Crawford and Romo. The first job I had with him was a sword fight. I was to double Steed and Romo and the boys would try to cut me into little pieces. I'm using my umbrella and they are using real swords. From the moment we finished rehearsing the routine I knew I was in safe hands with this lot. We used to go out together at nights to Birdland, which was a club on Wardour Street. A few drinks, meet the lads, pull a few girls. These were great times.

Romo worked with me on many projects over the years: *Raiders, Willow, American Werewolf, Bond*, we did it all. For many years Romo and Gerry Crampton would work as a team. Whatever job Gerry had Romo got in as his assistant. For a while they were called 'The King and I'. He was a lovely guy and I do miss him. I couldn't write anything about my life without including something in about this lovely man. Romo, wherever you are, mate, I love ya.

PAMMY

My darling wife or 'the current Mrs Taylor' as I like to call her was keen to put a few of her own feelings down for this project. Thank you Pammy, love you xx.

When I first met Rocky he was very much the man around everywhere and certainly a bit of a playboy (more than a bit actually). I could not believe how he kept going as I had no idea how tiring the life of a playboy could be and I actually, almost, felt sorry for him sometimes being so much in demand.

He would party in the evening (and into the night) and then had to be on a golf tee somewhere in the country early in the morning. He would drive John Virgo to snooker tournaments and then the races and there were always parties and film premiers or football matches.

Rocky is a member of the Variety Club Golf Society SPARKS and many others, including Jackie and Peter Allis's G.U.T.S (Guildford Undetected Tumour Screening) Golf Society. [Author's note: Peter Alliss is a former professional golfer, and is a television presenter and commentator, author and golf course designer] *Celebrities would put their names to these good causes and Rocky was always willing to help out going to La Manga, Majorca, Florida, Dubai etc. and travelled the length and breadth of the UK, Scotland, Ireland and Wales.*

When Rocky opened his nightclub, I think some of the film business thought he had retired, but far from it and the drinking until the early hours, playing golf, and general partying was interspersed with stunt work, including five months away in Mexico filming Titanic. *It was a crazy time and I don't know how he survived and I think his health was suffering. We sold the nightclub after seven years otherwise I am not sure he would be here to tell his tales.*

The local hostelry suffered when Rocky's opened, and the takings went down by a third, not from the absence of the locals, but because the clientele was from far and wide and they came for the karaoke, and also, I suspect because of the lack of Rocky's patronage!

However, the landlord John Huetson and his wonderful late wife Irene, continued to be great friends despite having introduced us!

When Rocky bought his nightclub that was the beginning of our relationship and I moved out of my home with my two boys into 'Rocky's'. This was very exciting for two young boys and their street cred rocketed. My eldest son James, who played rugby and is now a lawyer in Australia, was in awe of Rocky's skills as a stuntman and Nick my youngest was in awe of the film business and is now a film editor.

John Virgo rented my house in Cobham and my friend Rosie Ries was already in situ which made them 'flatmates'. That was twenty-five years ago and now several boyfriends and girlfriends later they are married – unbelievable. Rocky has been a real 'life force' for so many people, which is why he is loved by everyone.

Rocky's beautiful daughters Julie (Red) and Simone helped out at the beginning, but then moved on and got married. Red married Dan Dark (son of late John Dark who produced Casino Royale *and* Shirley Valentine*) on the* Eldorado *set in Spain. Rocky now has two very grown-up grandchildren, Bex and Tom, who are following in the families' footsteps in the film business and Dan, head of Warner Bros Studios UK, kindly donates prizes of Harry Potter outings for Rocky's golf tournament with John Virgo every year at Burhill in August.*

Simone's wedding took place in a marquee on the late Terry Yorke's farm. Rocky's friend Bob Patmore took Simone and Gary to change at the Hilton in Cobham in his helicopter and took Rocky's parents Larry (who came over from South Africa) and Pat for a ride over the countryside and they were thrilled with the experience. Simone has two gorgeous daughters, Taylor-Anne and Mollie, who are very grown up and pursuing their chosen careers.

JOHN VIRGO

Hello folks, JV here. Just wanted to hijack a chapter of Rocky's book to tell you a little about our friendship and why it's gone on for so long. What can I say about Rocky that hasn't already been said? For a start off Rocky Taylor can get you any phone number of anybody anywhere at any time. Not only that but I'll tell you how he does it later, too.

Here's an example of Rocky in action. One Saturday I was chatting to him on the phone. I'd told him that in an ideal world I'd have liked to have taken my son, Gary, to see the Manchester United v Crystal Palace game that afternoon at Selhurst Park. "Well, why don't you go?" says Rocky. I told him that it was a bit late to start hustling for tickets now and besides, it was advertised as a sellout. About four p.m. that same afternoon Rocky calls me back and says, "Right, I've spoken to Sir Alex Ferguson's secretary who has left two tickets for you at the players' entrance. Kickoff is at five forty-five p.m. so you've still got time to get down there. Enjoy."

I was lost for words. I thanked him, and my son and I set off for Selhurst Park. We arrived at the players' entrance and a doorman says, "Oh hello JV, he's bringing the tickets down himself." I thought, who does he mean? Who is he? Then in the doorway the doorman invites us in. There with my tickets is Sir Alex himself. "Hello John, is this your boy? I hope you have a great day. Here's the tickets for you." Now as surreal as this sounds I had met Sir Alex before at Old Trafford because I took five penalties in front of the home crowd for charity, but nevertheless this is classic Rocky.

I first met him many years before at Hampton Court Palace. Well, in the pub there called the Ferry Boat Inn. It was New Year's Eve 1984. We chatted briefly, and he came over and chatted with my mum. I brought Mum along as she always loved a good party, but was in a wheelchair which prevented her from letting loose. Rocky came over to her and asked her if she wanted to dance. She said she'd love to, so he wheeled her onto the floor and danced with her. Him standing and strutting his stuff and her sitting in her wheelchair having a ball. That was the first time I realized that this man was a really generous and lovely guy. To dance with Mum was a very sweet thing to do and it made Mum's night.

A whole year went by till I met him again, ironically the following New Year's Eve at The Tiberius Restaurant. A friend of mine who I'd invited along was a film fan, so was asking Rocky about his work and which stunts were the most dangerous. He told him that the fire stunts are always very difficult to work with. That always stayed with me as it was that coming June where Rocky would nearly lose his life in a fire stunt on Death Wish III.

The accident brought us closer together and during his rehabilitation we'd come up with a plan to go off and have fun together, playing snooker or beach combing somewhere. We stayed good mates right through this time and when he was back on his feet and looking for work the phone wasn't doing a lot of ringing. So, I'd say why not come down and play some golf with me? I'd get a pro-am tournament and get Rocky to come along. I was playing snooker tournaments and was also involved in the BBC show Big Break *so many more people would have seen me, even if they weren't dedicated snooker fans.*

As a spin-off to that show I did a few 'videos' to accompany the success of the show. Incidentally if you are under the age of twenty-five, you'll probably have no idea what a video is. So, to explain it was a rectangular DVD. So now you know.

Anyway, I got Rocky along as a guest on a few occasions. The show was called Go with Virgo, *a snappy title I'm sure you'll agree. It was me doing trick shots and showing Rocky and another celebrity guest how to perform them. One of my finest moments on that show was me playing an almost impossible cue ball that was sitting in Rocky's mouth. I say in it, but really it was sitting just on his puckered lips. The idea was to play the cue ball and watch it loop out of Rocky's mouth onto the table where it would kiss the black and drop delicately into the corner pocket.*

In reality what happened was I went to play the ball with enough power to get some lift and ended up jabbing him very hard in the cheek. His years of experience in screen fights kicked in and he parried my blow effectively, spitting the ball out onto the table. Part of me was very concerned that I had caused him some sort of injury and the other part of me could see that the cue ball was actually going to kiss the black. I could barely watch as contact was made and the black glided slowly but surely towards the corner pocket. It gently arrived at the corner pocket and plopped very satisfactorily onto the pocket. I was over the moon. Rocky as usual played down the whole thing and said he was fine, but when I got him on the next show he arrived bandaged from head to foot!

We had many great years on the road. Going from snooker tournament to snooker tournament and race course to race course. We both love horse racing and we are both partial to a flutter. I remember on one occasion we were having the worst day ever. Couldn't back a winner if someone paid us. We'd lost every race and so in a last-ditch attempt to save the day and redeem ourselves Rocky rang his mum, who many of you will know is a pretty decent tipster on a good day. Well, she gave us a horse, we backed it and naturally it stormed home pulling hand springs. Also, Rocky managed to get us into a very exclusive area of Newmarket races one day simply by being with me. I must say at this point that I have never used the phrase, "Do you know who I am?" But Rocky does it for me. He'll say he's with snooker player John Virgo and in we go. On this occasion we ended up in this lavish room. Wonderful food, champagne, cocktails. You name it and it was there. We ate, we drank, and we thoroughly enjoyed ourselves. We walked out passing what looked like a number of very serious-looking officials from the racecourse. Obviously scratching their heads and wanting to know who 'these two' were and why they had just eaten and drank a great deal of the banquet laid out for a party to welcome the Aga Khan, who was on his way up the stairs at that very moment. Rocky could barnstorm any location.

Another memory was again around the time of Big Break and my manager Troy Danton and Dave Dee, from Dave Dee, Dozy Beaky, Mick and Tich fame, had written a song about snooker and wanted me to record it in a studio in Liverpool. I was very excited and so was Rocky. As you all know by now he doesn't need an excuse to get up and sing a song. Providing it's one of the old favourites. I'm in the vocal booth getting ready for a take and out of the corner of my eye I see Rocky with the producer. Rocky says to him, "If he gets through this in one take can I do Green, Green Grass of Home for my mum?" Later on that night I'm booked to do a personal appearance at a working men's club in Liverpool. As I'm introduced onto the stage I hear the song I had recorded that afternoon being played over the speaker system. I turn to look at the bloke in the corner who is working the PA and see Rocky smiling back at me. He'd managed to get his hands on the master copy of the recording and had it on a cassette playing through the room.

I did mention at the start of all this that Rocky is a very generous man and I know this first hand from the occasions that I've been lucky enough to attend the Stunt Ball. An event put on periodically by stunt guys and girls to support charities of all sorts. The first year I went Rocky had been working in Ireland with the late great Peter O'Toole on a movie called High Spirits. Rocky and Peter were talking as Peter had been watching the news coverage of Rocky's accident very closely at that time in 1985. Peter asked him what he'd been doing lately. Rocky said, "I've been travelling around with John Virgo."

O'Toole's eyes lit up and his mouth dropped open. "John Virgo? Good God man he's my hero." Which was very gratifying. Turns out that Peter was a snooker nut. Loved the game and I was one of his favourite players on the circuit. "Does he like a bet?" asked Peter with a quizzical look in his eye.

"Yes, we both do," said Rocky.

Peter nodded. "Yes, I thought so. I can tell by listening to his commentary!"

Anyway, on the strength of this Rocky invites me and Peter O'Toole to that year's Stunt Ball at the Grosvenor House Hotel and the great actor sat next to me all night. Which was a joy.

But as with all the best things in life you must save the best till last.

At that event there was to be a raffle. Many lovely prizes had been donated by major companies and celebrities to be won in the raffle or auctioned off. To present the raffle was none other than Dame Vera Lynn. A stage was at the other end of the dance floor. She was announced, and the band struck up with We'll Meet Again *and* White Cliffs of Dover. *The audience joined in and gave her a rapturous welcome. Now if you've ever been involved in a raffle you'll know that it's either nail-biting stuff or over quite quickly. The raffle must have taken about half an hour, maybe more. And during this time those people who hadn't won anything were wandering off back to the bar. By the time Dame Vera had finished the raffle she just kind of walked slowly off toward the side of the stage.*

Again, I must add at this point that Rocky is an extraordinary character. A truly lovely man, but in moments of need his brain and mouth don't always read the same memo. Consequently, they often work against each other instead of together in harmony. This is a moment in point.

Rocky in a moment of genius rushes onto the stage and grabs the microphone. "Come on, ladies and gentlemen. Let's not let her go without showing your appreciation. So, come on let's hear it for Dame Edna!" Of course, the whole place fell about with laughter. I'm not sure Dame Vera saw the funny side, but everyone else did. In moments like this Rocky never realizes what he's said. So, he comes back over to the table and says, "Come on then, what have I done this time?" So, we told him. His face was a picture.

It's moments like this that make me very happy to know Rocky and his wife Pamela. In fact, they are responsible for me and my wife Rosie getting together in the first place. Rosie was friends with Pamela so we all shared a house for a while. Rosie and I have been together for twenty-five years thanks to Rocky and Pammy. He was best man at my wedding eight years ago. That's right, we waited eighteen years to get married. You can't rush these things, now can you?

I would also like to add that when Rocky had that accident back in 1985 he was very ill indeed. Physically he was banged up in a very bad way and mentally he was struggling too. All because of a movie.

The payout he received from the court case wasn't a substantial sum of money. In fact, if you look at what he'd been through a few hundred thousand pounds seems like a drop in the ocean. If this had taken place in the United States, he would have walked away with possibly many millions of dollars in compensation and been given an alternative shot at a future outside of the stunt business. We've all done whatever we can to get him work, but personally I feel that the way his case was dealt with was very unfair indeed.

It's periods in Rocky's life like this that again go to show how great he really is. After all this he bounces back and now has a chance to leave a legacy that people can read and enjoy for many years to come.

It has been my pleasure to know him and I sincerely hope we have many more years of laughs and good times to come.

[Author's note: I wanted to add this story about John from those days when we were out on the road. One day John comes into the room and say's "Why aren't you ready?"

I looked down at myself and said "What?!"

John was clearly a bit annoyed by my answer. "What do you mean *what*? Why aren't you in black tie?"

Again, I looked round the room looking for inspiration or a clue... something that would help me answer John's question. "Why would I be in black tie, John?"

He was now really angry. "Why would I be in black tie? What sort of a question is that? Because I'm in the final and I need you to be in black tie. It's official Rocky, that's just the way it is."

I swallowed and said, "I haven't got a dinner suit with me, John... I haven't got black tie."

John was fuming and snapped at me, "WHY NOT?"

I looked at the floor, kept my head bowed and looked up at him with just my eyes. "Well, I didn't bring it because... I've never been to a final with you before... I didn't think I'd need it." I laughed... John didn't.]

THE CHANGES I'VE SEEN

As with anyone who's been in a particular line of work for some time, you start to see just how much the business has changed. I mean, take turning up for a job on set. You'd get a phone call a day or so before and then you turned up ready to work. Nowadays if you're new to the business there are so many hoops you have to jump through in order to get on set. We have a thing called an observation day where new register members can visit the set and the coordinator will give them jobs to do on set, it also means they can meet other members of the crew and stunt team. And this can only happen after you've called almost every coordinator on the register and begged for an afternoon or day on a real TV or film production.

There is also the months of rehearsing that takes place. I know it's important, safety is our priority after all, but everything takes so long nowadays. Back in the sixties and seventies you'd turn up on set and the coordinator would say, "Okay Rocky, you're doing the car turnover and then this afternoon I need a motorbike lay down." You'd nod and say, "Righto, Guv." Then get on with your day. Now the scene has been partly arranged by CGI. You turn up to find that majority of the sequence will require you to drive the car from point (a) to point (b) then the CGI car will take over and do the crash into the tree. Same with high falls. I wasn't much of a high fall man. I did a few at forty to fifty feet but some of the big guns back in my day like Roy Alon and Terry Forrestal would regularly do 100 feet plus. The last UK stuntman to do a 100-foot fall was Daman Walters on *Assassin's Creed*. He did 125 feet. Then in the final cut of the movie the fall looked less somehow because of everything else that was going on.

Stunt coordinators now employ fight arrangers because of the many different types of fighting style available. Again, in the sixties, seventies and eighties the stunt coordinator coordinated the action single-handedly. We have more assistant coordinators now than ever before on films and certain TV shows, too. This is inevitable as life changes then film should change too. In some situations, the production team neglect to change where change is necessary. The most recent Jackie Chan movie *The Foreigner* is a good example. The fighting style is predominantly martial arts-based. But one of the characters is an Irishman. Now, without a back story it seems awkward and a little out of place for him to be fighting in the same style as everyone else. They thought about this and did some re-shoots. Now the Irish fella weighs in with fists and furniture instead of the way of the dragon.

If you were young and up and coming you'd be taken under an old professional's wing. He'd show you the ropes and give you advice. With me it was Peter Diamond, he gave me my first big break. I was lucky I had my dad too who'd been in the business for years. Greg Powell had his dad Nosher, a tower of strength and experience. He could act too and got many heavy roles. When he was a kid his dad, Nosher, was working on *From Russia With Love* back in 1963. Greg was a child of eleven but, when he visited the set, he'd fetch this and carry that for the other stunt guys. Make tea that sort of thing. Old stuntmen like Fred Haggerty would say "Here, go and fetch my gun, eh?" Greg would go and pick up Fred's weapon and bring it to him. Health and safety would have a fit these days if they knew that a child was allowed to get within fifty yards of a loaded weapon. But it was different times. Back in 1967 when *You Only Live Twice* was in production at Pinewood, Bob Simmons was really struggling to find the quantity of men to fill the positions of ninjas for the climactic battle sequence. They would go to gymnasiums and hire guys that did karate, or guys who were good at gymnastics. They even hired one or two lads who had done a stretch inside. The reason they were so agile was because they'd had plenty of experience as a cat burglar! There was no paperwork to fill out, apart from initial registration with the casting director and then you didn't need to give a real name. I knew a few lads who in those early days just went by nicknames and nobody knew anything about them at al,l and yet they were on every picture. I remember Terry Yorke introducing me to a guy I knew as Jeff. He was on a couple of shows and films then never saw him again. These guys come and go. Some are in for the long haul and some get in by accident. Some of the guys from *You Only Live Twice* have been living off their stories of turning up for a day's work then being told they were too fat or not right for the part, for the last fifty years.

Today's stunt performer has wanted to be a stuntman or woman since they were born. The moment they were delivered by the doctor they wanted an adjustment fee and demanded a re-take otherwise they might not get paid at all. They know all about the business before they get in, they study the art of action at college and university and are in touch with their inner selves.

We didn't have any of this. I always make the connection between *The Sweeney* and showbusiness. Regan and Carter are on a massive all-night whiskey bender, which involves a few pints as well, hours down the casino and then on the way home they pick up a couple of stewardesses who work for British Airways. They go back to Regan's place, have it away with the two young ladies, wake up the following day with the mother of all hangovers and then through sheer determination, dedication and their own body weight in cigarettes manage to save the day, catch the bad guys and get a commendation from the commissioner.

Also, there are people brought in to perform stunts these days because of their skills. Some skills that existing performers may not possess. On *Skyfall* there was a brilliant motorcyclist called Robbie Maddison. His ability with a bike is second to none and he is Daniel Craig's double throughout that brilliant pre-title sequence. I can ride a bike, I've been riding bikes all my life, but I can't ride one like him and that is where these guys come in. On another Bond, *The World Is Not Enough,* we had a world champion powerboat racer called Sarah Donahue take the wheel of a beautiful Sunseeker boat to chase up and down the Thames. We didn't really have these guys back in my day. You did as much as you could do. If a film required a hand-gliding expert,

225

then unless someone on the register possessed those skills you'd have to come up with another method of getaway for the hero. Roller skating maybe. Then we could all sit back and let Roy Scammell do it.

In a nutshell, that is what we did in the business every night for over twenty years. And you'd never know because we could act. I remember Eddie Eddon on one of the Superman movies standing outside a petrol station that had just blown up. The flames were hundreds of feet high and, as the camera passed by, Eddie could be seen throwing a bucket of water on it. The fact that a bucket of water wouldn't have made the slightest bit of difference isn't the point. The fact is that he did something. Far too many people these days are put in TV shows or films and are just standing there.

Michael Caine always told the story about how when, as a young actor, he was cast in a local amateur production. The scene rolled on and the director brought the scene to an end. He walked over to Michael and asked, "And what are you doing in this scene?"

Michael smiled and said, "Oh nothing, sir."

The director was scarlet with rage. "And why not?"

Michael looked him in the eyes and said, "Well I have nothing to say, sir."

The director then came and sat next to him. "You have many wonderful, beautiful and exciting things to say, but in this scene, you must show the audience that you are choosing not to say them." What many people forget is that to be a stuntman you must qualify to be an actor. Which means you must understand and adapt the script the way any other actor would. Alongside your stunt requirements – if you have any, that is. You do see stunt guys and girls from all over the world cast in movie and TV roles and on occasion they appear to have forgotten that they are actors.

I was one of those lucky few who was in the right place at the right time. And I am of a certain generation where you could have a great time on set and take a liberty or two along the way.

Sir John Mills said to us, me and Greg Powell on the set of *Sahara*, "Boys you do a fine job," and do you know what? That is all the praise you require. If an actor, best boy or receptionist takes the time to say "Well done" you know you've done all right.

I'm lucky as I have one of those faces that everybody seems to remember. People in the street come up and say, "Hi Rocky, how are you?" Or they tell you about their favourite film that I was in or my dad was in.

And yet the official bodies in this industry like BAFTA and the Academy of Motion Pictures, Arts and Sciences, who have awards every year still don't recognize stunt performers with any award. Why?

There is a BAFTA for 'Best Sound' and an Oscar for 'Best Hair and Make-up', but the movie which has the best sound and the best hair and make-up is often sold by the action in the trailer. Guess who does the action? Yes. The stunt performers. Car crashes, high falls, fights, fires, horse riding, jumping, running, even standing still. We do it all. All in order to make the actors and actresses look great on screen.

Take the action out of the James Bond films or the Indiana Jones movies or the Batman pictures and what have you got? Firstly, you'd have a very short movie and secondly it wouldn't be very exciting. And excitement sells. Adverts on TV these days for bread have budgets of small movies and employ stunt people to give the product an exciting edge over its competitors. So again, I ask you what is wrong with creating an award for the stunt artists to say thank you? It doesn't have to be through the medium of a little golden statue, but that would be lovely.

An industry award for 'Best Stunt Coordinator/Ensemble' would do. We're not asking for much. I won a Screen Actors Guild award for being part of the Stunt Ensemble for *Fast and Furious 6* which we filmed in Majorca and here in the UK. Now if SAG can do it why can't other major organizations?

FAST AND FURIOUS 6

I was asked by Greg Powell if I fancied six weeks in Majorca on a movie? Would I, I thought? In this business you have ups and downs. You are self-employed and must find the work where you can. I'd had a dry spell, a job here a job there, but the time between the two was getting longer. Then Greg called, and I was back in the game. Sometimes fate drops out of a clear blue sky and lands in your lap.

So, I packed and away we went. We had a brilliant time. It was a wonderful time to be working and a fine project to work on. For those of you who have been living under a rock for the last ten years, the *Fast and Furious* series had gone from strength to strength, going to many exotic locations and pulling in billions of dollars at the box office. So, we went to Majorca, London, Glasgow and Liverpool. Yes, Liverpool and Glasgow! These were the locations used for a number of the car stunts. The car turnovers in the tunnel were filmed in the Mersey Tunnel in Liverpool and the cooperation received from the city council was second to none.

The big tank chase down the freeway was done in Majorca and I was driving one of the many cars avoiding the oncoming tank. But I also managed, on this movie, to fulfil one of my childhood dreams. I got to fly a C120 cargo plane. Well, I say fly... it was in fact a large furniture truck that had been gutted and dressed to look like an aircraft. I got to drive it down the runway and the chaos and action took place either inside it or around it.

The sequence on screen was questioned by some as being overlong, which in hindsight it probably was, but it wasn't half as long as that runway!!

Some boffins at a university worked out that if you take the speed of the vehicles and the length of the sequence, on screen, you can work out how long the actual runway would have to be. Well they calculated that the runway would have to have been at least thirty-five miles long for all of this to have taken place. Even pilots were convinced that it actually happened for real. Greg was leaving his house one day and a neighbour, who was a pilot for Ryanair, asked him where in the world this runway was as it's what every pilot dreams of landing on. Size isn't everything, but I guess when you're a pilot the length of your runway is a big deal.

BOBBY DAVRO

Bobby has been a wonderful addition to the world of comedy since 1981. He was a major part of Saturday night TV and had his own shows throughout that decade. He still packs them in wherever he performs today. He's also a mate and as I've already mentioned that is very important to me. Here's Bobby to tell you more.

Rocky's, the night club in Cobham, was the first time I met the great man. I was brought there by Richard Sandham who, as it happens, was a very talented judo instructor. I went there as did the rest of the population of the country because of the karaoke nights. Which were legendary. Such a brilliant turnout. You could go on a midweek night and they'd be queuing out of the door. Over time singing at the karaoke turned into doing a turn. I am a comic singer so any excuse to sing a song and have fun with it was right up my street.

He doesn't need an excuse to sing a song himself you know... of course you know which song, right? He has a very commanding tone to his voice and great stage presence. Just like Hitler.

I'd get up there have a laugh and joke, take the mickey out of anyone and everyone including him and his mum, bless her. He would turn up at the venue when he could, but of course often he would be filming somewhere and couldn't be a stable fixture. He was very badly injured as you know, working on a movie in London.

I used to do a gag about him by saying, 'You know we all love Rocky, but he's not the sharpest tool in the box sometimes. On that stunt from the burning building they're all stood at the bottom holding a blanket shouting, "Come on jump, we'll catch you."

'Rocky looks down and says, "I know what you buggers are up to, put the blanket on the ground. Then I'll jump."'

Course when he got to the hospital he was in a very bad way. His doctor was a woman and she said to him, "Look Rocky, I'm sorry but you're going to have to stop masturbating."

He looked at her and said, "Christ, Doctor, why?"

She said, "Because I'm trying to examine you!"

Also, he's very good at giving other people a chance. It doesn't matter where in the world they are from, he is happy to help them out. Take right now he's got a cleaner from the old Eastern Bloc, but she is going to have to go. It took her five hours the other day to hoover the living room... Yes, folks she's a Slovak.

And you have to turn the tragic moments into the funny moments. He may have already told you about the night that the club got raided by masked gunmen. Poor Pammy was in the place as Rock was away and the gunman burst into her bedroom. He grabs hold of the sheet and pulls it from a very nervous Pammy hiding under it. He looks at her lying there. She looks up at him and says, "Are you a rapist?" He looks down awkwardly at her and says, "I am usually. Just put some clothes on."

Rocky is always there. If you need something he'll do whatever he can to get that done for you. You can rely on him and that is really important in this day and age. Rocky thank you for everything. Bobby x

231

THE LAST RUN

THE LAST WORD

This job entitles you to see and do many things that anybody would most certainly dream of. In 1971 I did a movie called *The Last Run* with George C. Scott.

I'd been a fan of his for many years, so to get an opportunity to work alongside him was a big thrill. I doubled him in the driving sequences and played a role as a heavy. I've talked about this for years to anyone who cared to listen but hadn't seen the movie for twenty-plus years. Someone asked me recently how I felt about being dubbed in the final edit. "I am?" I was shocked, surely they were mistaken.

Turns out they were right – I walk into shot with my gun pointing at Mr Scott and then say my line – only it isn't my voice that came out. It was very Italian. Now I have been known to dabble with an accent from time to time, but Italian isn't one of them.

I was mortified for a moment or two… in fact an hour or two. I mean I'm in a scene with George C. Scott and nobody hears my actual voice! I mentioned this to a few people I know in the biz. They call it 'DVS'. Which stands for 'Darth Vader Syndrome'.

I felt the same way that poor Dave Prowse did back in 1977 during the premiere of *Star Wars*. He took his mum and family with him and they all discovered for the very first time, as Vader said his first line, that he'd been dubbed by James Earl Jones. Poor bugger! He was destroyed. Understandably as he'd filmed the whole picture, including all the dialogue. When he moved, in the costume, he seemed to float, which was an added bonus to Vader's evil side. The only drawback to his excellent physical performance was the fact that Dave was very proud of his West Country accent. George Lucas had decided that if Darth Vader was to be as menacing as he could be on screen he would need to have a voice that everyone would remember the very moment they heard it. Sadly, for Dave it just wasn't his voice.

I felt that. I understood his pain, but I've accepted the fact that at the time if I'd been in the dubbing suite I could have argued the point. Alas, I wasn't. So, I have to live with the voice they used for me after all.

I also had a nice little stair fall in that picture which they managed to cut too. You can't win 'em all, eh?

MACGYVER MEETS ROCKY

Macgyver was a TV show that back in the mid to late eighties was doing great business in the US. Regularly with a prime-time slot, good ratings meant all boxes were ticked. As with many US shows they will often film an episode on location. In this instance it was here in England.

I was part of the stunt team and managed to get a role. Yes! An acting role. I played a character called 'Plato' who discovers our hero, played by Richard Dean Anderson, walking along a roadside trying to avoid a police roadblock that has been set up for him. After some… interesting dialogue [Author's note: I actually use the phrases 'Plates of meat' as in cockney rhyming slang. 'Plates of meat' = feet and 'Couple of freezers' as in 'fridge-freezer = geezer.] The stunt coordinator was Martin Grace who put me forward for this role. I remember going to the audition. I walked into the room to be faced with ten people! I was surprised to see so many people in to cast an eye over the audition. "Good morning, Rocky. You've read the script?"

I told them I had but needed to add something. "Can I ask who wrote this script, because it's shit?"

A deathly hush fell in the room. One man pointed down the length of the table. "He did," said the man.

A stern looking man was eying me over the rims of his glasses. "Yes, I wrote it," he said.

I had to think quickly. "In that case it is without question one of the very best scripts I think I've ever read." The room fell about laughing. "I imagine that's me off the list then?" I enquired.

The producer looked at me and said, "We'll let you know, Rocky. Thank you for coming in."

I'd convinced myself that I'd done it again. Put my foot in it. Half an hour later I got a call from the audition to say the role was mine.

My major scene was for MacGyver to run around the back of the police roadblock out of sight. And for me to cause a diversion, which I did with rock music pumping out of a ghetto blaster balanced on the tank of the motorcycle. I then realized why they needed a stuntman to ride the bike. To avoid suspicion, I ride away from the roadblock and part way up the road out comes MacGyver from the trees. I step off the bike as it's rolling along, he gets on and then I get on behind him, then grab the handlebars. From the road the police, if they wanted to look would only see me on the bike. Just to be on the safe side I brought in stuntman Phil Lonergan to double our hero.

I only did that sequence, but it was great fun to do and Richard Dean Anderson is another very nice guy.

RUSSELL HOWARD

Russell Howard is a very funny comedian who has been a regular fixture on the BBC for many years. I was asked to do one of his shows called *Good News*. One of the features in the show is where he gets someone along who he knows nothing about and interviews them. On this occasion I was that person. A fairly straightforward thing. He interviews me, finds out what I do, then we do a little bit of business for the audience. But he knows nothing about me. With other people they might be the world's greatest Rubik's Cube expert or have a photographic memory. But with me this is very different. I'm a stuntman and if I am to show Russell what I do, I must do this physically.

I had gone through the routine with the floor manager, producer and director, but Russell was kept in the dark. So, showtime and he asked me a few questions to try and guess why I was sitting on the same stage as him, but he didn't get it right. So, I introduced myself and the audience were right behind me which was great for the added tension and excitement in the room. I told him we'd work out a little fight routine where I punch him, he'd react, then hit me with a sugar glass bottle, then after getting a piece of breakaway furniture round my earhole I'd throw him through a window onto a nice soft landing.

First part went well. He was very excited about having a go and was in the process of doing some form of stretching exercise then he leaned on the breakaway table. Being made of balsa wood and cut through, it just couldn't hold his weight and he crashed to the floor. As with anyone in the same situation he put his hands out to stop himself. His wrist took the full weight and landed awkwardly. He lay there for what seemed like an eternity. The audience thought we'd started the routine and laughed loudly. The problem was that poor Russell was actually in very serious pain. He'd broken a finger and we had to stop the routine for a while, so he could get the finger strapped and dressed. Now usually that would be the end of it, but Russell has big balls and was never going to let the audience down. He arrived strapped up, in pain but very keen to please. We went through a stripped-down routine and he threw me through the window in the end. But honestly what a trooper. The 'good news' on this occasion was that Russell lived to fight another day and maybe has second thoughts about a career change, too.

PERSUADED TO FALL DOWN STAIRS

As you get older you realize that there are some things you just can't do anymore.

I believe it was Clint Eastwood in the *Dirty Harry* movies who said, "A man's got to know his limitations." Well he was dead right. As a stuntman, knowing what you can and can't do is going to be a very important part of your day-to-day existence and physical stunts, after a while, do start to take their toll.

Falling down stairs, as you've already read, was something I used to do a lot of. In my prime it was something I enjoyed very much. You still padded up just in case but the key to a good stair fall is momentum. Once you go, that's it. Next stop is the bottom.

I've done a few good ones over the years. One I was pretty keen on was on the last episode of *The Persuaders.* Roger as Lord Sinclair is searching a house for clues. He hears footsteps, he turns and runs out of the room where he finds a private investigator played by actor Donald Pickering leaning up against the wall as he'd been shot.

Cut to me as Donald's character falls and I gave it hell for leather down the stairs. Only at the last moment did I give my head a proper 'WHACK' on the wall. The director, Peter Medak came over and said, "Well done, Rocky, that was marvelous." The truth was that while he was stood there, I saw four of him, the world was spinning, and I was hoping I wasn't going to throw up.

I heard myself saying, "Would you like it again, Guv?" I prayed inside that he'd say no as I don't believe I could have given him another take, not after the first one. Luckily, he said no. I loved that show.

I did a couple of episodes for Les Crawford and John Sullivan. Les was a brilliant double for Roger. I did mostly fights and falls. I also did an episode with Dad. It was called *Chain of Events* and saw Danny, Tony Curtis, handcuffed to a briefcase containing, or so they think, official secrets that the Russians and MI5 are after.

The final scene takes place in an old house and a fight breaks out. Me and Peter Brace are caught up in it and, for just over minute, I am thrown about by the leading lady Suzanna Leigh whilst Tony Curtis looks on and applauds.

The last one was an episode called *The Time, The, Place* and involved me falling down more stairs with Terry Plummer in a TV studio where someone is trying to kill the Prime Minister, while Ian Hendry and his radicals try to take over the country.

An early Brexit ploy foiled, you might say. Art imitating life?

LEWIS GILBERT

During the writing of this book we learnt about the passing of a very fine British director.

Lewis was a lovely man. Although I only worked with him on two occasions, watching him work taught me a lot. On *You Only Live Twice* we, me and the other gathered stunt performers, sat in the volcano set which had been built on the backlot at Pinewood Studios watching Sean Connery, Lewis Gilbert and stunt coordinator Bob Simmons going through the upcoming scene. His instructions to us came via Bob and we would then prepare ourselves to die in a number of ways for the camera. Once the shot was got Lewis would come over and say to us all, "Well done, stunt boys, that was very good." Which I've always respected in a director.

Ten years later I got to work with him again on *The Spy Who Loved Me.* Lewis was very good to me and selected me as one of the guards that would escort James Bond (Roger Moore) and Major Amasova (Barbara Bach) whilst on *The Liparus* tanker. I worked alongside Jimmy Lodge and we got an opportunity to watch Lewis craft a performance from Curt Jurgens which was very exciting to watch.

He was also a very funny man who took an immediate liking to pretty much everyone on set. The on-set antics between him and Roger are of course legendary, and they remained friends over the next forty years. At least they are together again now. Roger delivering the funny one-liners and Lewis shooting it with three cameras to make sure that the editor had all the best shots.

A good example of what Lewis was like was told to me by stuntman Roy Alon. He was on *The Spy Who Loved Me* and was given the role of one of the detained submarine crew. During the ensuing firefight, he throws a grenade and is shot with a blast of machine-gun fire. Well, that's how the shot was supposed to go. After a dry run-through everyone was in place for a take. Background action kicks off and Roy is given his cue. Comes into shot, hits his mark, pulls the pin on the grenade and throws it. You hear the burst of machine-gun fire and Roy throws himself dramatically to the floor. Sadly, for him it turned out that the special effects man had got a problem with the blood squibs attached to Roy's chest. [Author's note: For those unaware a blood squib is a bag of fake blood which is activated by an electrical charge provided by the special effects team and fired remotely.] Only one of them had gone off and it was one that was quite close to his shoulder. The other five had refused to go off. Roy had died very dramatically... from a flesh wound.

Later that day Roy found himself talking to the editor John Glen about the scene. John took him to the editing suite and ran the sequence. A few frames into the action and in walks Lewis. "Ah John, can you cut just after the grenade is thrown and before the gunfire goes off, please? I'd like to keep Roy in the scene, he's come all the way from Yorkshire to be with is." Lewis referred to Yorkshire like it was Timbuktu!

But that was Lewis. A fine director, a fine professional and a really nice fella.

HIDDEN CAMERA STUNTS

On occasion I've been asked to do a *Candid Camera*-type show, where the public is the star. Then back in the eighties Roy Alon had organized a prank to be played on stuntman Billy Horrigan for the show *Game for A Laugh*. Billy's car, his pride and joy, was substituted for one of the action cars in the sequence. Everything was going well until Billy recognizes the car crashing in front of him. Of course, Roy had found an identical car and the TV show crew had painted it to make it look like Billy's. So, from time to time you get involved in these things. But when you take the public away and replace them with actors it becomes more controlled. It also becomes a bit more elaborate.

Stewart James got me on as assistant coordinator and we set up shop in this hotel in Morocco. The actress who was to get 'pranked' was called Shaimaa Saif and the set up was to be a prank based on *The Towering Inferno*. Just think about that for a second. A practical joke based on a burning building! What people do for a laugh these days is unbelievable.

Anyway, we had a bunch of stunt people working on it including Phil Lonergan, Tony Van Silva, Matt Stirling and Tracey Caudle, Elaine Ford and Donna Williams. The plan was to have Shaimaa Saif in her penthouse suite and the building catch alight. We'd put stuntman Guy List in the room as one of her security detail. All of ours guys were wearing earpieces, so they could hear the presenter who would ask them to do certain movements during the show, which was filmed live. The only person who had no idea what was going on was the star, Shaimaa.

242

We had top special effects guys, running state of the art fire rigs which were concealed behind the walls of this building. Stunt guys and girls running around, getting set on fire, getting blown up by explosions. It was full on. How this poor actress who knew nothing about the whole thing didn't die of a heart attack was beyond me. My heart was in my mouth watching the action live and I'd arranged it. It was a serious piece of practical joking and only one you could away with on a big budget.

We did three weeks doing a number of shows for this production company. One was with Paris Hilton in an out-of-control helicopter and the other was with an Italian actress who went out on a boat trip with some unsuspecting guests for a film festival. She then jumped into the water and was eaten by a shark. In actual fact a diver picked her up about twenty feet down and took her to safety, but not before another diver swam by with a fin on his back and had left a trail of blood in the water. When they prank people, they do it for real.

Pranking has come a long way since the old, Bob Monkhouse *Candid Camera* sketch where a man drives onto the forecourt of a garage and says he is having trouble with the car. The mechanic opens the bonnet to find that the engine is missing! The producers didn't then decide to blow the garage up. That's the difference between then and now.

STUNT SPEAK THE LANGUAGE OF ACTION

I'm often asked about how we create action for film and TV. Back in the day a few basic facts would have been enough, but nowadays the audiences are more sophisticated and want their action to be much more realistic. Which means they require much more information about the 'how' and the 'what'.

Nice and easy to start with. Let's look at cars and turning them over.

The ramp is the traditional way of jumping a car or motorcycle. To turn a car over using a ramp you had to approach it and get two wheels on. If you get all four on you just jump instead of roll. So, two wheels only on the ramp, then at the end of the ramp, as the car is leaning, you flick the steering wheel left or right, depending on which way the car is to roll. By flicking the steering one way or the other (and here's the science bit), the weight of the vehicle plus the rapid change in direction causes the over balancing and ultimately the car will roll. Got it? Right, now with that in mind, let's look at the next stage to the ramp roll.

Nowadays turning a car over isn't as complex as watching the ramp and getting both wheels on before the roll. These days you drive your car at a metal pipe and it turns over. The pipe roll was an American invention and was used extensively in film and TV before coming over here in the early eighties.

The pipe looks like a ramp only you don't drive your wheels up it. You simply straddle it. At the end of the pipe is a thing we call a kicker. This is the key to how high you can go. It's a steel pipe with a steel doorstop-type thing welded on the end. I've done a few and they are very spectacular. The last one I did was at the O2 arena when I got myself into the record books. In 1985 stuntwoman Dorothy Ford became the first female stunt performer to successfully use the pipe ramp for a car stunt. She won that year's stunt challenge programme. It's still one of the very best car turnovers ever.

A pipe ramp is also easier to hide. I mean on set. So, the ramp can be placed in the middle of the road if you like. Park a car in front of it and it's concealed. With a ramp you had to be a bit more creative by building a market scene around it or having it inside a building so the car would be seen flying out through the windows, for instance.

One more step from the pipe is the cannon. Yes, you heard me correctly a cannon roll is, I believe, the most exciting way to turn a car over. What is a cannon, Rocky? Well, I'm glad you asked me that. A cannon is a device that is placed inside a vehicle by the special effects team. Its job is to fire an object, could be part of a telegraph pole or a metal pole onto the ground. How do you think it does this? No, not by gunpowder or explosive, but that's an excellent guess. It uses compressed air or nitrogen. The force of this leaving the underside of the car and jabbing into the road causes the car to flip over. Its resting place can sometimes only be decided by which way the wind is blowing.

If you remember the sequence in the first Daniel Craig Bond movie *Casino Royale*, Bond is chasing the bad guys in his Aston Martin when he arrives at speed over the brow of a hill to find his Bond girl lying on the ground with her hands tied. He swerves to avoid her, and we see the car lift onto two wheels then roll uncontrollably down the road. The stunt driver was Adam Kirley and originally the stunt crew were to use a ramp. But the Aston is a clever car. Everything about its design and inner workings tells all the on-board computers that it is not going to get its wheels off the ground. Therefore, it does everything in its power to prevent a roll.

They decided that a cannon would be a better way to control the roll. Adam drove the car at nearly seventy m.p.h. and, at the given moment, he slid the car and punched the button on the handbrake that would trigger, engage and fire the cannon. Seven rolls later Adam found himself several hundred feet down the road and in the pages of the *The Guinness Book of Records*.

We should now take a look at the cars themselves. They are road-going vehicles, but the one that is driven by the stunt driver is often very different to the one being driven by the actors. For a start the stunt vehicle will have to be stripped of its interior. All the seats must be removed. The gearbox may need to be adjusted so the gear-stick may need to be replaced. A roll cage will be put inside the vehicle to strengthen the body of the vehicle when it rolls. This cage will be built to the stunt driver's own specifications. He will work with the special effects teams and tells them exactly where he wants everything to be. Where does he want padding for the roof, where he wants the driving seat to be? That sort of thing. After all the stunt driver must be kept safe. This roll cage will prevent the bodywork, roof etc. from being crushed and injuring the stunt driver.

The petrol tank will be drained and often bypassed so that a fuel cell can be used instead. This will contain just enough fuel for the vehicle to perform the stunt. If the script requires the car to catch fire, then the special effects team will rig the vehicle to ignite. It won't catch fire due to a fuel spillage.

As I mentioned, the interiors will be removed but a racing seat is put in place of the driver's seat. This will support the stunt driver's back along with his protective clothing. He'll wear a neck brace and his helmet will have a locking system attached. This can be secured to the seat which will prevent his head from being whipped forwards or backwards causing injury.

I used to get plenty of motorbike jobs too, so we should take a look at them. One of my favourite stunts with a bike is where we see the bike crash into an oncoming or stationary vehicle causing the rider to fly over the handlebars and onto the road or through a window. Now, anyone who has ever fallen off a motorcycle will know that it's not graceful. It's ugly, noisy and over in the blink of an eye.

In order to recreate this type of crash for a film or TV show the motorbike must be modified. The rider must be able to clear those handlebars without injury to the shins. So, the foot pegs are moved to just underneath the seat. This allows the rider to push off and clear the handlebars and keep looking where he is going to land. Often a landing area has been prepared for him. Funnily enough the landing often depends on where the rider is looking just before the impact. Keep looking straight ahead and you'll leave the bike in a straight Superman-type position. Look down and you'll hit the floor much faster than you anticipated.

The other way I've come off bikes in the past is with the 'lay down'. This is created by squirting the power on with the throttle, turning sharply to kick out the back wheel and adopting a speedway-type slide which causes you and the bike to part company. Done at speed it can be very exciting indeed. In many cases the road is either covered in water first or pea shingle or small handfuls of gravel are scattered on the floor to assist the slide. Again, this is done to the stunt rider's requirements.

Ever since I can remember I have loved horses. There was a time in this business where if you didn't ride a horse you didn't work. We were doing period pieces, and all required good horsemen. The fistfight is often considered a stuntman's bread and butter, but back then it was horses. These are some of the most exciting moments as a stuntman. Unlike a car or motorcycle, a horse has a mind of its own. If on the day of shooting the sequence the horse decides he/she doesn't want to do it, nothing will change their mind.

As a rule, these animals are on their very best behaviour and do an amazing job, which is why they are so sought after the world over. Let's look at the saddle fall first. The key to this is the stirrups. We use a type of stirrup called an L-step. It's shaped like the letter L and made of metal. This makes it easier for the rider to push away from the horse when he is reacting to being shot. This way he won't get tangled in the stirrup and get dragged by the horse… unless required to do so, that is.

Bringing a horse down (falling) can be done a few ways. Firstly, we use the reins to guide the horse to the floor. They are trained for three to four weeks to respond to one rein or the other being pulled. We then tie the rein off and repeat the process. They turn their heads in such a way that they go past the point of no return and overbalance causing them to fall. Every time they do this we give them a carrot. They do it over and over getting carrot treats every time. Again, the stirrups are very important here and are made of leather so when the horse lands they fold up without any injury. We call them cup stirrups. Your foot sits in comfortably and can be removed quickly without snagging.

A breakaway is often referred to when talking about props. In particular about furniture, which can be used in fight scenes. Real furniture is replaced with balsa wood furniture which is lighter. It is cut in such a way that talcum powder can be put into the cuts in the wood. When the item is broken over the back of an actor or stunt performer it breaks much easier and allows the performer to react accordingly.

The Air Ram. This is a very special piece of kit which allows the super power of flight. Well, kind of anyway.

You've watched those war movies where a grenade is thrown, or the soldiers run into a minefield? One or all of them are blown up and thrown through the air by the force of the explosion. In the old days we would use a full-sized or mini trampoline to get enough height. Nowadays the stunt professional uses the air-ram. It is small, compact and can be buried into the ground. It works on high pressure compressed air. The only requirement is that the stunt performer steps on the plate at the right moment, causing it to propel them through the air and either onto a box rig or down onto the ground.

While we are talking about compressed air we should mention the ratchet. Again, back in the day we called it a jerk harness. It's another method of dragging or pulling someone from point (a) to point (b). Either on foot or horseback as we used to do with our jousting troupes.

Now then, as you will have noticed, I am not averse to being set on fire. All in the line of duty you understand. It is the most dangerous of all the stunts a performer will be asked to undertake. Why? Because there are so many different elements involved. So many possible pitfalls that could mean the difference between life and death. You must rule everything out before embarking on a fire. There are two types of fire 'gags'. Stunts are called 'gags' in the business. The first is the partial body burn. As the title suggests you set fire to a portion of the body. The arms or the leg, but nothing else. Firstly, a cooling gel is applied to the area to be burnt. The actor Joe Pesci had his head set alight for the *Home Alone* movie. An experience he described as "One of the worst things I've ever had to do." He was in safe hands and had nothing to worry about, but fire does that. It creates a sense of unease.

In this instance the gel was applied to Joe's head, then on top of that a flammable substance was applied. The science is that the cooling slows down the rate at which the flammable gel burns, which allows the stuntman or actor to perform the moves or say the lines. This flammable gel used to be called 'barbecue sauce'. This name has been frowned upon by the community and rightly so.

The full burn is a much larger exercise. Think of it as the partial body burn on every part of the body. The key, apart from the gel we looked at earlier, is layers. Regardless of the size of the burn a performer must be layered up.

Onto the skin goes something a bit like thermal underwear only it's soaked in protective gel. Then on top of that goes a racing driver's fire suit. More protection. On the top of that goes a protective layer that will prevent the fire suit getting burnt and then on top of that goes the costume, whether a hat and coat, or whatever.

We have a code set up as the stunt performer can't communicate with us during the take, so we put in place a set of movements, so we can understand what's going on. Let me explain that. The performer is set alight. They will have a routine to go through whilst on fire. Walk from here to over there and turn. When they decide they are feeling the heat through the many layers they will drop to their knees. When they want to get put out they lay flat and we go in and put them out.

I've done one or two and they are very dangerous, exciting to watch though and incredibly noisy. The sound of fire burning your costume is one I don't think I'll ever get used to.

Nowadays when I say the word 'bulldogging' I'm looked at like I'm trying to promote sexual activity in car parks and fields full of cows. But you must remember that I am 'old skool', and the phrase comes from the Old West and the days of wrangling cattle.

Picture the scene. The hero, on horseback, is chasing the gunslinger. He must catch up with him and stop him before he gets to the town to rob the bank. So, our hero rides up next to the gunslinger, jumps from the saddle of his horse, grabs the villain and takes him and occasionally the horse to the ground. This is bulldogging in all its movie glory. Cowboys used to use this method to wrestle a steer to the ground by leaping from a galloping horse and grabbing the steer by its horns before bringing it to the ground.

We talked earlier about the world of CGI and how it can enhance some of the stunts that are performed these days. High falls are such an area. We mentioned about Damian Walters being one of the last stunt performers to actually fall over 100 feet for a movie. Well, back in 1981 Vic Armstrong had developed a thing called the fan descender which would allow stunt performers to fall great heights under the control of the special effects team. It was used to great effect when Roy Alon was doubling an actor who was to fall from the main city bank in Rio for the movie *Green Ice*. The first eighty to ninety feet of the fall was on a fan descender and the next 100 feet was Roy falling into an airbag. Still to this day it's one of the greatest falls I've ever seen.

Roy used to make the airbags that we fell into. Before he joined as a stuntman, he was Roy Wilson [Author's note: Roy had to change his name as there was already a Roy Wilson registered with Equity. Alon was his stage name and was the name of his then wife Nola spelt backwards] and Wilson's airbags were the very best. He'd done enough falls to work out what was required and how they would improve the safety of the performer.

The airbags had arrived from the States, but when they were used over here for the first time, they were quite unforgiving. Vic Armstrong did a jump one day from a tower on a picture. The pressure in the airbag needed to be just right to support the stunt performer's weight as they hit the bag. Vic hit the bag, but the pressure was wrong. It pitched him up and forward and he landed in the car park.

With the introduction of CGI the high fall can be made much bigger, but you still need a stunt performer to do the first part of the fall. Consequently, falls in movies are now 3-400 feet with the stunt guy doing the first forty to sixty feet and the CGI doing the rest.

As you will have noticed from this section many terms and 'speak' will have changed by now. In fact, the language of action changes on a daily basis because action changes on a daily basis. In fact, if we get the opportunity to do all this again I doubt very much that any of us will be able to understand a single word that anyone is saying. But I guarantee the fight in the bar will be first class.

AND FINALLY

I have been very lucky to be in a career that allows my face to become well known. I have one of those faces that people just recognize.

I remember an occasion in a supermarket one day when I'm going about my routine pushing the trolley with the wonky wheel and I get the feeling I'm being followed. Not by another shopper but more a stalker. Anyway, I've been up tinned foods and am minding my own business halfway down men's toiletries when this woman taps me on the shoulder. I turn and face a little old lady. I ask what I can do for her. "It is you, isn't it?" she asks as I reach for an extra-large antiperspirant.

"Yes, that's right," I said already rummaging for a spare pen to sign whatever she wants me to sign.

The smile dropped from her face. "In that case would you mind telling me when you intend to come back and finish the bathroom?"

I swear there are so many occasions where people mistake me for someone else because they know my face.

Oh, and I really should tell you about the *Delilah* and Tom Jones thing, shouldn't I? On a number of occasions during this book there has been more than a passing mention to me getting up somewhere and singing *Delilah* or *Green, Green Grass of Home*.

It's really quite simple. I know *Delilah* inside out and back to front. To me it's like the Lord's prayer. Something I can recite without having to learn it. I can do that with many of Tom Jones' numbers. His range and mine aren't a million miles apart and because of that I can get away with singing songs by Elvis and Englebert without having to change a key or re-arrange a tune.

I'm also asked why I choose to sing a song that 'condones murder'. Well, if you want to believe that the song is about a Welshman spying on his girl who he catches in the act with another and then chooses to kill her with a knife after breaking in the door, then so be it. However, a great many people, millions I would say are happier to remember this tune as a song that evokes great memories about when you heard it first and what you were doing at the time. Too many people overthink everything these days which, as you can tell from this, then overcomplicates everything else.

I sing because I love to. I have a passion for a tune. Nobody complains when I sing *My Way* by Frank Sinatra, do they? And they say, "Well you can't have Delilah's lyrics on your tombstone, now can you?" I don't know though. Would it be wrong to have 'Forgive me Delilah I just couldn't take any more' as a strap line across the face of the grave? I suppose many people would want something on the stone that connects them with the work they have done during life. Spike Milligan had the funny line 'I told you I was ill' written across his and the actor Jack Lemmon simply had 'Jack Lemmon in' written on his.

After the life I've had and the things I've seen I'm not entirely certain where I will end up. Up there? Or down there? If it's up there I can finally rest among the great and good of the entertainment world. Catch up with old friends and remember the good times. But if it's down there I'll open a club. I've done it before. Why not then? Late licence, no admission fee, wine, women and song. The story of my life, eh? And what will they say when they see my name on the list to join them in the eternal fire? Simple they'll all shout 'JUMP ROCKY, JUMP!'

THANK YOU

This is where I say thank you to each and every one who has ever been in my life. Well, if I did that we'd be here until volume two of my memoirs comes out at the cinema.

But seriously, there have been so many people who have been so influential in my life. So many who have come into my life, sometimes only briefly but have made a difference. I can't name all of them, but I can remember where I am today and what I've had to do to get here. So, to all of you, I thank you.

First my family. Whatever goes on in your life you always return to your family. I'm lucky my mum is a trooper and has always been the very definition of independent. Long before the Spice Girls and the 'Girl Power' revolution, my mum was standing up as a breadwinner. She taught me a lot and has always given me the love as only a mother can. My beautiful daughters, Julie and Simone, keep me going. I wasn't always there as I was away working a lot, but what I missed out on then we've made up for since. My late wife Wendy was with me from the start. We'd come such a long way together that when she died prematurely I thought I wouldn't be able to carry on, but she did give me a great deal of strength in those last few weeks. Which is ridiculous when you think about it as I should have been giving her the strength and support. My cousin Roy and Sue and my Pammy for everything and so much more.

Dear friends Rosie and John Virgo who made this book possible and also to Jon Auty for being enough of a fan to know more about me than I know about me.

Following my accident on *Death Wish* – Marlena for being there every day. Greg Powell, Vic Armstrong and all the stunt boys, too many to mention, thank you, thank you for my benefit night at Pinewood, without which I would not have survived. All the stunt coordinators who have been good enough to employ me for a day or night or six-month shoot. Also, the many pals who visited me in hospital and who helped me on the road to recovery including Derek Burrows and Nigel Pearce who were the first to come in with champagne and a mini basketball game. Even though I had tubes everywhere we managed to sip some champers and attempt a slam dunk. Many thanks too to the doctors and nurses of St Thomas' hospital without whom I would not be here to tell the tale.

And again, I must thank the many thousands of everyday folk who cared enough to send flowers or cards to the hospital at the time. I read each and every one and I am eternally grateful.

FILMOGRAPHY

2019 *Angel Has Fallen* (utility stunts) (pre-production)

2018 *Johnny English 3* (stunt driver) (post-production)

2016 *The Legend of Tarzan* (stunt performer)

2016 *Ramez Plays with Fire* (TV Series) (assistant stunt coordinator – 5 episodes)

2016 *Pranking Antonio Banderas* (assistant stunt coordinator)

2016 *Pranking Dina Mohsen & Shaimaa Saif* (assistant stunt coordinator)

2016 *Pranking Ahmed "Mido" Hossam* (assistant stunt coordinator)

2016 *Pranking Ghada Adel* (assistant stunt coordinator)

2016 *Pranking Ragheb Alama* (assistant stunt coordinator)

2016 *I Golden Years* (stunt driver)

2015 *Avengers: Age of Ultron* (stunt performer/stunts)

2014 *Robot Overlords* (stunts)

2014 *Hercules* (stunts)

2014 *Death in Paradise*, TV series, (stunt coordinator – 1 episode - Episode #3.4 (2014) ... (stunt coordinator)

2014 *Jack Ryan: Shadow Recruit* (stunts)

2013 *Closed Circuit* (stunt performer)

2013 *World War Z* (stunt performer – uncredited)

2013 *Fast & Furious 6* (stunts)

2013 *Utopia,* TV series, (stunt coordinator – 1 episode)

Episode #1.6 (2013, stunt coordinator)

2013 *The Wee Man* (stunt coordinator)

2012/I *Ashes* (stunt driver)

2012 *Jab Tak Hai Jaan* (driving stunts)

2012 *Skyfall* (stunts)

2012 *Cockneys vs Zombies* (stunt performer)

2012 *The Hot Potato* (stunt player)

2012 *Tezz* (stunt driver)

2012 *Wrath of the Titans* (stunt performer)

2012 *Cleanskin* (stunt double)

2012 *John Carter* (stunts)

2012 *Safe House* (precision driver)

2012 *Plastic Gangsters,* TV movie, (stunt coordinator)

2011 *Sherlock Holmes: A Game of Shadows* (stunt performer)

2011 *Unwatchable,* short, (stunt coordinator)

2011 *Johnny English Reborn* (stunt performer)

2011 *One Day* (stunt performer)

2011 *Harry Potter and the Deathly Hallows: Part 2* (stunts)

2011 *Game of Thrones*, TV series, (stunt performer – 2 episodes)

2011 *The Pointy End* (stunt performer)

2011 *You Win, or You Die* (stunt performer)

2011 There Be Dragons (stunt coordinator)

2010 *Harry Potter and the Deathly Hallows*: *Part 1* (stunts)

2009 *Dead Man Running* (stunt coordinator)

2009 *Doghouse* (stunt coordinator)

2009 *Looking for Eric* (stunt performer)

2008 *Abraham's Point* (stunt coordinator)

2008 *Getting Out*, short, (stunt coordinator)

2008 *Richard & Judy,* TV series, (stunt coordinator – 1 episode)

- Episode #1.1 (2008) ... (stunt coordinator)

2008 *Frankie Howerd: Rather You Than Me*, TV movie, (stunt performer)

2008 *The Oxford Murders* (stunt performer)

2008 *Honest*, TV series, (stunt coordinator – 2008)

2008 *Caught in the Act* (stunt coordinator)

2007 *National Treasure: Book of Secrets* (stunts: London unit)

2007 *Dolphins* (stunt coordinator)

2007 *Rise of the Footsoldier* (stunt coordinator)

2006-2007 *New Tricks*, TV series, (stunt coordinator – 2 episodes)

2007 *Casualty* (stunt coordinator)

2006 *Lady's Pleasure* (stunt coordinator)

2007 *Back in Business* (stunt coordinator)

2006 *Big Nothing* (stunt coordinator)

2006 *The History Boys* (stunt double: Hector)

2006 *Children of Men* (stunt performer)

2006 *Stormbreaker* (stunts)

2006 *Doctor Who*, TV series, (stunt performer – 1 episode)

2006 *The Idiot's Lantern* (stunt performer)

2006 *The Da Vinci Code* (stunts)

2005 *V for Vendetta* (stunts)

2005 *BloodRayne* (stunt coordinator)

2005 *Dead Fish* (stunt driver)

2005 *The Golden Ho*ur, TV series, (stunt arranger – 1 episode)

- Episode #1.4 (2005) ... (stunt arranger)

2004 *The Defender* (stunt coordinator)

2004 *The Phantom of the Opera* (stunts)

2004 *Reel Race*, TV series, (stunt coordinator)

Waking the Dead, TV series, (stunt coordinator – 4 episodes, 2001 – 2004) (stunt performer – 2 episodes, 2001)

Fugue States: Part 2 (2004) ... (stunt coordinator)

Fugue States: Part 1 (2004) ... (stunt coordinator)

Every Breath You Take: Part 2 (2001) ... (stunt coordinator)

Every Breath You Take: Part 1 (2001) ... (stunt coordinator)

Burn Out: Part 2 (2001) ... (stunt performer)

Show all 6 episodes

2004 *The Mysti Show*, TV series, (stunt coordinator)

2004 *The I Inside* (stunt coordinator)

2004 *Sea of Souls*, TV series, (stunt coordinator)

2003 *Faking I,* TV series, (stunt coordinator – 1 episode)

- *Faking it... as a Stuntman* (2003) ... (stunt coordinator)

2002 *Anazapta,* video (stunt coordinator)

2002 *The Importance of Being Earnest* (stunt double)

2002 *Alone* (stunt coordinator)

2002 *Mrs Caldicot's Cabbage War* (stunts)

2001 *The 51st State* (stunts)

2001 *The Mummy Returns* (stunts)

2001 *In Deep*, TV series, (stunt coordinator)

2000 *Shiner* (stunts)

2000 *House!* (stunt coordinator)

2000 *Bomber,* TV movie, (stunts)

1999 *The World Is Not Enough* (stunts – uncredited)

1999 *The Mystery of Men*, TV movie, (stunt coordinator)

1999 *Shergar* (stunt performer)

1999 *Plunkett & Macleane* (stunt performers: additional photography)

1998 *Elizabeth* (stunts)

1997 *Tomorrow Never Dies* (stunts)

1997 *Incognito* (stunts)

1997 *Titanic* (stunts – uncredited)

1997 *Keep the Aspidistra Flying* (stunts)

Pie in the Sky, TV series, (stunt coordinator – 6 episodes, 1996 – 1997) (stunt arranger – 3 episodes, 1996) (stunts – 1 episode, 1995)

Return Match (1997) ... (stunt coordinator)

Cutting the Mustard (1997) ... (stunt coordinator)

Gary's Cake (1996) ... (stunt coordinator)

Breaking Bread (1996) ... (stunt coordinator)

Chinese Whispers (1996) ... (stunt arranger)

Show all 10 episodes

1996 (stunt coordinator)

1996 *Michael Collins* (uncredited)

1995 *The Governor*, TV series, (stunt coordinator – 6 episodes)

- Episode #1.6 (1995) ... (stunt coordinator)

- Episode #1.5 (1995) ... (stunt coordinator)

- Episode #1.4 (1995) ... (stunt coordinator)

- Episode #1.3 (1995) ... (stunt coordinator)

- Episode #1.2 (1995) ... (stunt coordinator)

Show all 6 episodes

1994 *Shopping* (stunts)

1993 *Son of the Pink Panther* (stunts)

1993 *The Mystery of Edwin Drood* (stunt coordinator)

1991 *Bergerac*, TV series, (stunt coordinator – 1 episode)

- *All for Love* (1991) ... (stunt coordinator)

1991 *Robin Hood: Prince of Thieves* (stunts)

1991 *Highlander II: The Quickening* (stunt double: Ramirez)

1990 *Paper Mask* (stunts)

1990 *Nuns on the Run* (stunts)

1989 *Boon,* TV series, (stunt performer – 1 episode)

- *Love Letters from a Dead Man* (1989) ... (stunt performer)

1989 *The Return of Sam McCloud*, TV movie, (stunt coordinator)

The Bill, TV series, (stunt arranger – 1 episode, 1989) (stunt coordinator – 1 episode, 1988) (stunt driver – 1 episode, 1987)

- *Time Out* (1989) ... (stunt arranger)

- *Tigers* (1988) ... (stunt coordinator)

- *Overnight Stay* (1987) ... (stunt driver)

1989 *Indiana Jones and the Last Crusade* (stunts)

1989 *Slipstream* (stunts)

1988 *High Spirits* (stunt performer)

1988 *Without a Clue* (stunts)

1988 *Buster* (stunts)

1988 *Who Framed Roger Rabbit* (stunts)

1988 *Willow* (stunts)

1986 *Biggles* (stunts)

1985 *Spies Like Us* (stunts)

1985 *Death Wish 3* (stunts)

1985 *My Beautiful Launderette* (stunt coordinator)

1985 *Invitation to the Wedding* (stunts)

1984 *Ordeal by Innocence* (stunt driver)

1984 *Indiana Jones and the Temple of Doom* (stunts)

1983 *The Secret Adversary*, TV movie, (stunt advisor)

1983 *Never Say Never Again* (stunts – uncredited)

1983 *Curse of the Pink Panther* (stunts)

1983 *Krull* (stunts – uncredited)

1983 *Octopussy* (stunt double: Roger Moore – uncredited) / (the stunt team)

1982 *Victor Victoria* (stunts)

1981 *Brideshead Revisited*, TV miniseries, (stunt rider – 1 episode)

- *A Blow Upon a Bruise* (1981) ... (stunt rider)

1981 *An American Werewolf in London* (stunts)

1981 *Raiders of the Lost Ark* (stunts)

1978-1980 *The Professionals*, TV series, (lead stunt double – 4 episodes)

The Acorn Syndrome (1980) ... (lead stunt double)

Blind Run (1978) ... (lead stunt double)

Long Shot (1978) ... (lead stunt double)

Killer with a Long Arm (1978) ... (lead stunt double)

1980 *Safari 3000* (stunt coordinator)

1979 *Blake's 7*, TV series, (stunts – 2 episodes)

- *Countdown* (1979) ... (stunts – uncredited)

- *Hostage* (1979) ... (stunts – uncredited)

1978 *Superman* (stunts – uncredited)

1978 *The Wild Geese* (stunts – uncredited)

1977 *The Spy Who Loved Me* (stunts – uncredited)

1977 *A Bridge Too Far* (stunts – uncredited)

1977 *Stand Up, Virgin Soldiers* (stunt coordinator)

1976 *The New Avengers*, TV series, (stunt double – 1 episode)

The Eagle's Nest (1976) ... (stunt double: Gareth Hunt – uncredited)

1976 *Confessions of a Driving Instructor* (stunt coordinator) / (stunts)

1975 *The Sweeney*, TV series, (stunt performer – 1 episode)

- *Stoppo Driver* (1975) ... (stunt performer)

1974 *The Man with the Golden Gun* (stunts – uncredited)

1971 *Villain* (stunts – uncredited)

1969-1970 *Randall and Hopkirk (Deceased)*, TV series, (stunt double – 26 episodes)

The Smile Behind the Veil (1970) ... (stunt double: Mike Pratt)

You Can Always Find a Fall Guy (1970) ... (stunt double: Mike Pratt)

Vendetta for a Dead Man (1970) ... (stunt double: Mike Pratt)

The Trouble with Women (1970) ... (stunt double: Mike Pratt)

It's Supposed to Be Thicker Than Water (1970) ... (stunt double: Mike Pratt)

Show all 26 episodes

1969 *Monte Carlo or Bust!* (stunt driving team – as Rockie Taylor)

1969 *The Champions,* TV series, (stunt double – 17 episodes)

Autokill (1969) ... (stunt double: Stuart Damon)

The Gun-Runners (1969) ... (stunt double: Stuart Damon)

The Final Countdown (1969) ... (stunt double: Stuart Damon)

Nutcracker (1969) ... (stunt double: Stuart Damon)

Full Circle (1969) ... (stunt double: Stuart Damon)

Show all 17 episodes

1966-1967 *The Avengers,* TV series, (stunt double – 2 episodes)

Dead Man's Treasure (1967) ... (stunt double: Patrick Macnee – uncredited)

Small Game for Big Hunters (1966) ... (stunt double: Patrick Macnee – uncredited)

1967 *The Dirty Dozen* (stunts – uncredited)

1967 *You Only Live Twice* (stunts – uncredited)

1963 *From Russia with Love* (stunts – uncredited)

ACTOR

2012 *The Hot Potato*

Thug 1

2009 *Harry Potter and the Half-Blood Prince*

Pedestrian (uncredited)

2007 *Back in Business*

Boris

2006 *Are You Ready for Love?*

Van driver

2005 *BloodRayne*

Monetary guard

2002 *Die Another Day*

Man, at Sword Club (uncredited)

2002 *Anazapta* (Video)

Compte de Fugiere

2001 *The Mummy Returns*

Man, in Alley (uncredited)

2000 *Sexy Beast*

Raymond

1999 *The World Is Not Enough*

Man, in restaurant (uncredited)

1999 *The Last Seduction II*

Gabriel

1997 *Tomorrow Never Dies*

Carver's thug (uncredited)

1997 *Titanic*

Bert Cartmell

1994 *MacGyver: Trail to Doomsday*, (TV movie)

Plato

1993 *The Mystery of Edwin Drood*

Head Ruffian

1992 *Blue Ice*

Patrol car driver (uncredited)

1989 *The Paradise Club*, (TV series)

Getaway driver

Bring on the Cavalry (1989) ... Getaway driver

1989 *Batman*

Napier Hood

1987 *Boon*, (TV series)

Minder

Special Delivery (1987) ... Minder

1985 *Dempsey and Makepeace*, (TV series)

2nd. Warder

Hors de Combat (1985) ... Second warder

1984 *Pull the Other One*, (TV series)

Harry

Grandma Does It Herself (1984) ... Harry

1984 *Smith & Jones* (TV Series)

- Episode #1.4 (1984)

1983 *Sahara*

Kamal

1983 *Never Say Never Again*

Hostage guard (uncredited)

1982 *The Jim Davidson Show* (TV series)

Episode #4.5 (1982)

1981 *Raiders of the Lost Ark*

German soldier (uncredited)

1979 *The Dick Francis Thriller: The Racing Game* (TV series)

Second heavy

Trackdown (1979) ... Second heavy

1979 *Blake's 7* (TV series)

Albian rebel / Federation trooper

Countdown (1979) ... Albian rebel / Federation trooper (uncredited)

1978 *The Wild Geese*

Mercenary (uncredited)

1977 *Candleshoe*

Hood (uncredited)

1977 *The XYY Man* (TV series)

Motorcyclist

The Missing Civil Servant (1977) ... Motorcyclist

1976 *The New Avengers* (TV series)

Soldier/ Cybernaut

Dirtier by the Dozen (1976) ... Soldier (uncredited)

The Last of the Cybernauts...? (1976) ... Cybernaut

1976 *The Pink Panther Strikes Again*

Asylum attendant (uncredited)

1976 *Confessions of a Driving Instructor*

Monks Hill rugger team

1975-1976 *The Sweeney* (TV series)

Thug / Flying squad officer

Selected Target (1976) ... Thug (uncredited)

Supersnout (1975) ... Flying squad officer (uncredited)

1976 *My Brother's Keeper* (TV series)

Motorcyclist
Have a Go (1976) ... Motorcyclist
1976 *The Slipper and the Rose: The Story of Cinderella*
Prince's Guard
1975 *Oil Strike North* (TV series)
Friend
Shore Leave (1975) ... Friend
1974 *The Man with the Golden Gun*
Beirut thug (uncredited)
1973 *And Now the Screaming Starts!*
1973 *Psychomania*
Hinky
1966-1972 *Doctor Who* (TV series)
Stunt guard / Egyptian warrior
The Curse of Peladon: Episode Four (1972) ... Stunt guard (uncredited)
Golden Death (1966) ... Egyptian warrior (uncredited)
1971 *The Persuaders!* (TV series)
Schubert's Man 2
Chain of Events (1971) ... Schubert's Man 2 (uncredited)
1971 *The Last Run*
Second man
1965-1968 *The Avengers* (TV series)
Mercenary / Mitchell / Student / ...
Have Guns – Will Haggle (1968) ... Mercenary (uncredited)
Escape in Time (1967) ... Mitchell
A Sense of History (1966) ... Student (uncredited)
Castle De'ath (1965) ... Gillie (uncredited)
1967 *The Dirty Dozen*
Airborne soldier (uncredited)
1961 *Top Secret* (TV series)
Second thug
The Disappearing Trick (1961) ... Second thug
The Young Ones (1961)...Youth Club thug